aw

ake

B

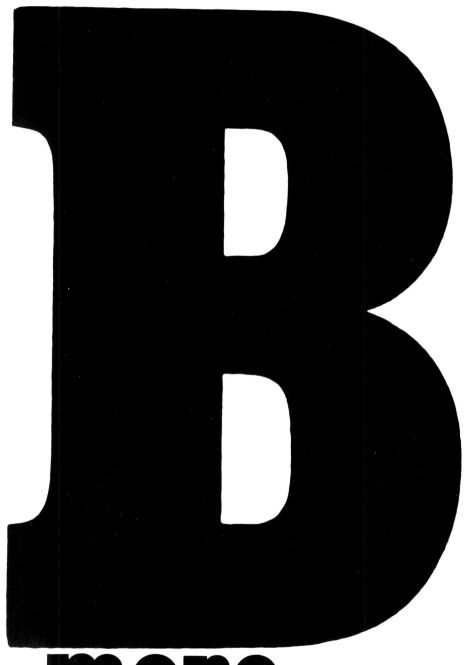

more

yourself

you limit yourself
unlimit yourself
limit less

energy consciousness

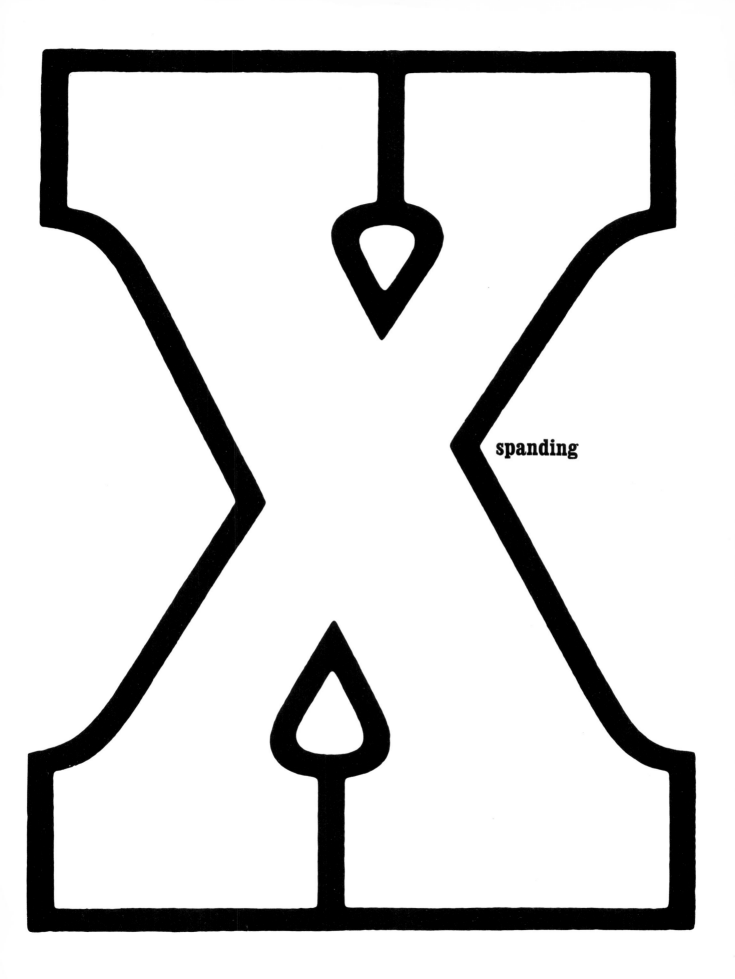

spanding

you can be
in and outside
of your experience
feeling sensation
mind/body/ALL
at the same time

**aware
of all a round
you**

**now
here
this**

**very
moment**

**you
are**

life

dancing

clouds
people
thoughts

ocean
emotions

changing
exchanging
interchanging
rearranging

on
and
off

birth

breath

death

**loves
metaphysical
comedy**

symphony
mind/body/spiritual
harmony

so **B** it

WHAT TO DO TILL THE MESSIAH COMES

By
Bernard Gunther
Photographed by
Paul Fusco

The Macmillan Company, New York, New York

The Macmillan
Company
866 Third Avenue,
New York, N.Y. 10022
Collier-Macmillan
Canda Ltd.,
Toronto, Ontario

Library of Congress
Catalog Card Number:
77-156844

First Printing

Designed by
William Hopkins

Printed in the
United States of
America

joy/us

celebrations

awareness experiments

thought
energy
massage
breathing
love
meditations

non drug ways
to grow flow on

for jacques hondorus

ed
ike and
mike

and the pure white light

much many special thanks: sharon wang-laurie nisson

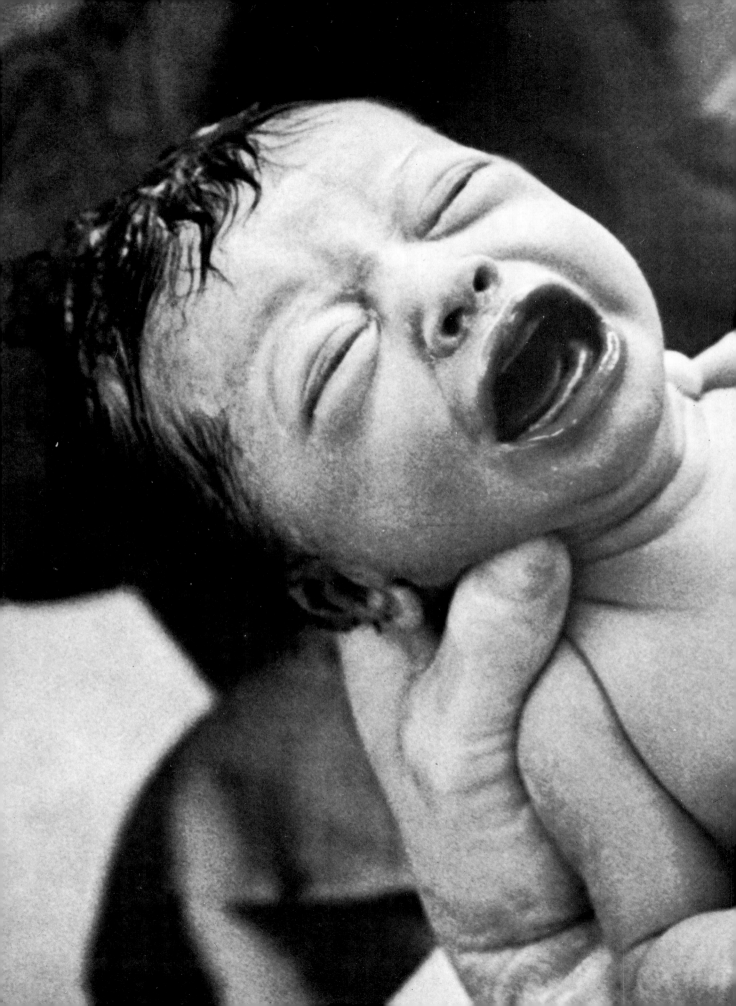

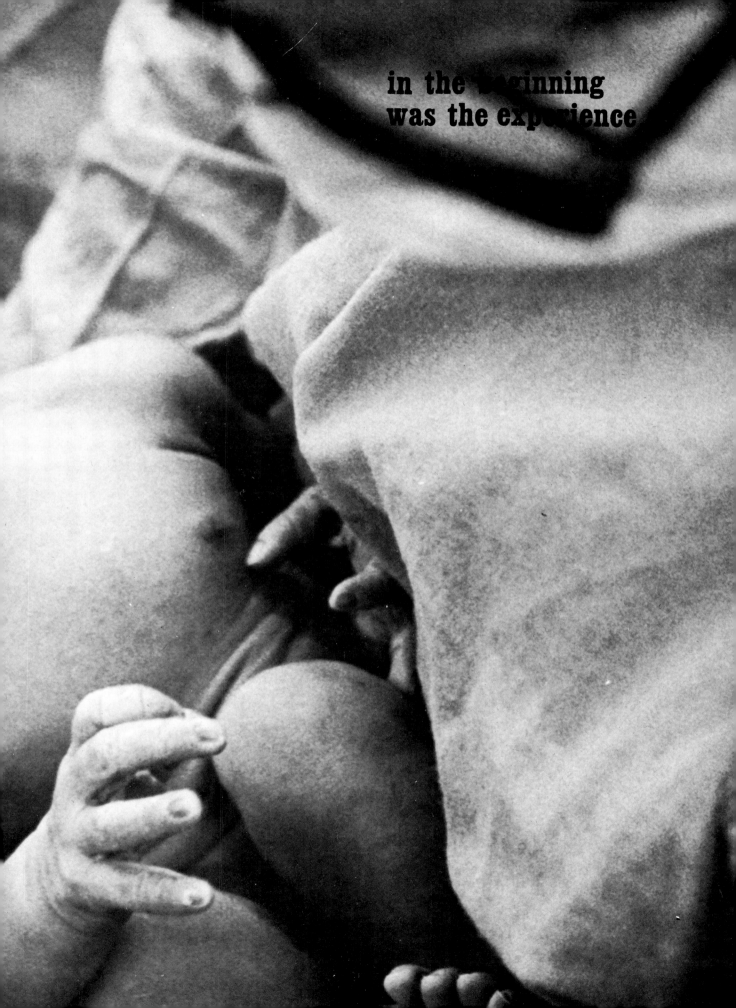

in the beginning
was the experience

total unity
alive
in every sense

in the
non/be/ginning
was the word

and the word
because god

creating separateness

I identify

he and me
me and not me
yours and mine

words are abstractions

symbols

hypnosis

conditioning
limiting
inhibiting

in
other
letters
words

any thoughts
pictures
images
you (ego) have
of yourself
or the world
may be useful
or harmful
but they are untrue
not really the

world
you

trance
end

reawaken
through
awareness
experiments
celebrations
food
massage
love
meditations
reflecting
energy
breathing
chanting
sleep
non-verbal
communication

stop the
frustration

hallucination
return

be
reborn

reincarnation

the ability
to flow
in and out
of conceptual
thinking

become again
like little children

child like
rather than
childish

each every
moment

a present

aware

to not
be aware
is no aware

awareness

is being

conscious
consciousness

alive
awake

in every sense

sensing

experiencing

each action
reaction

situation
moment

satisfaction

waking up laughter
───────────────────

after
waking up
before getting out of bed
stretch
your entire body
and then for
meditation breathing fun
laugh for 1
or 3 or 5 minutes

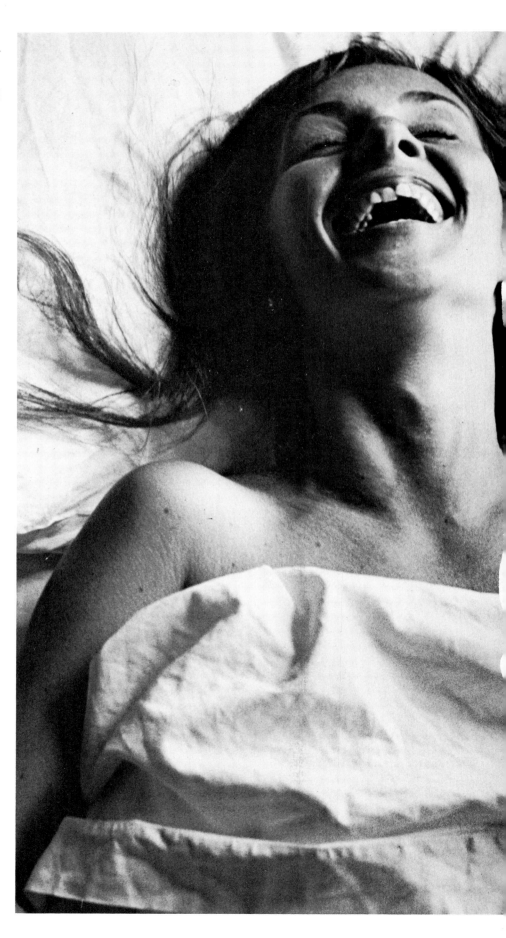

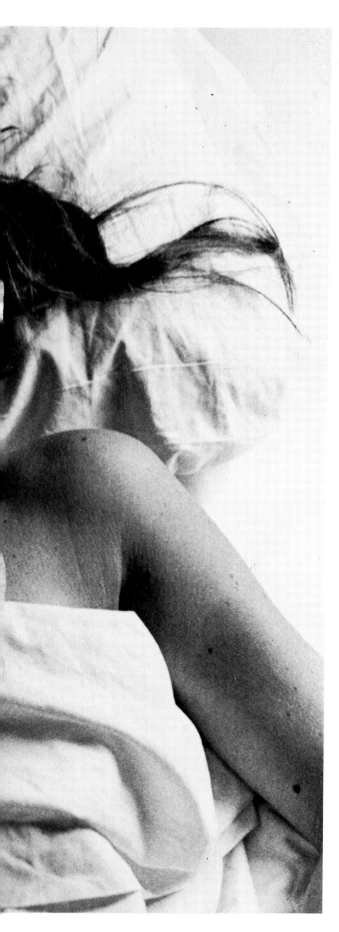

moment of tooth

take 5 minutes
to close your eyes
think about your
teeth and what
they mean to you
then open your eyes and
really give your teeth
a good brushing
move up and down
over the teeth and gums
the inside upper and
lower teeth and gums
the side of the wisdom
teeth do some of it with
your eyes closed
after a time switch
hands and do it
with your opposite hand
open your eyes
and take some dental
floss and clean
between your teeth
finally with a mouth
wash really gargle
close your eyes again
and experience how
your mouth feels

auto/suggestion

experience how
you get in and out
of your car
now slowly
get in your car
adjust your posture so
you are sitting easy
on your sitting bones
your back is straight
without being stiff
feel turning on
the ignition
listen to the engine start
its sound
then consciously slowly
take the brake off
and take off

you don't have to drive
your car yourself
all you have to do
is steer

be aware while you drive
if you feel the need
run your consciousness
over your body
start with your feet
calves knees thighs
hips back stomach
chest shoulders
arms forearms hands
neck face scalp
eyes
widen your eyes
3 to 6 times
each time hold them
for a count of ten
then experience
how you are

become aware of your
breathing
while waiting at a
stop sign
or do your
kagel lifts

rest in peace fully

close your eyes
and find
within your
body/mind
a serene scene
feel picture
experience in detail
a special
refreshing place
in the mountains
or at the sea shore
your own island
planet or heart cave
an inner space
where you can go
any time you need
to get away
stay in the place
for 1 to 5 minutes
or as long as you
need to
when you're ready
leave slowly
open your eyes
realize this place will
be there anytime you
want/need to return

rest

be

peacefully

all factoring

close your eyes
and with just your finger
gently slap your nose
for from 15 to
30 seconds
take your hands away
and experience
how your nose feels
next sensitively place
your left little finger
into your left nostril
as far as it will
easily go
let it stay there
for 15 to 30 seconds
take the finger out
and exprience both
nostrils
then place the little
finger of the right hand
in the right nostril
after 15 to 30 seconds
take the finger out
and experience both
nostrils
now open your eyes
and go on a smell trip
around the house
food
perfume
spices or
go outside and smell
individual trees
flowers the grass
nature

what it sounds like

with your finger tips
tap all around your ears
then with the palm/heel
of your hands
very lightly pat
the ears themselves
after close your eyes
and experience
how you feel
then slowly and gently
place one of your
left fingers in
your left ear
after 15 to 30 seconds
take the finger out
and experience
both ears
now place one of your
right fingers in
your right ear
after 15 to 30 seconds
place both fingers
in both ears
after taking them out
experience how you feel
how everything sounds
after close your eyes
and from 3 to 5 minutes
just focus listen
to the different sounds
that surround you
in a room
on the street
an automobile
or plane
coming
and going
the voices of people
animals
your own voice
body
breathing
music
nature

orange juice see/taste

see feel
smell touch
an orange
then put it down and
very slowly cut it
experience the cutting
listen to the sounds
see the juice come out
look at both halves
the design
the flesh
cut a round slice
and hold it up
to the light
see the design
of the fibers
now squeeze the orange
listen to the sound
see it drip
its color
its pits
bubbles
now pour it
into a glass
close your eyes
and slowly drink
the juice

you nut T

take just one
of your favorite nuts
close your eyes
and eat slowly
in extremely small bites
(4 or more per nut)
after taking a bite
don't take another
until you have
completely chewed
and liquified
swallowed the last
when you have
finished the nut
keep your eyes closed
and experience
the after taste

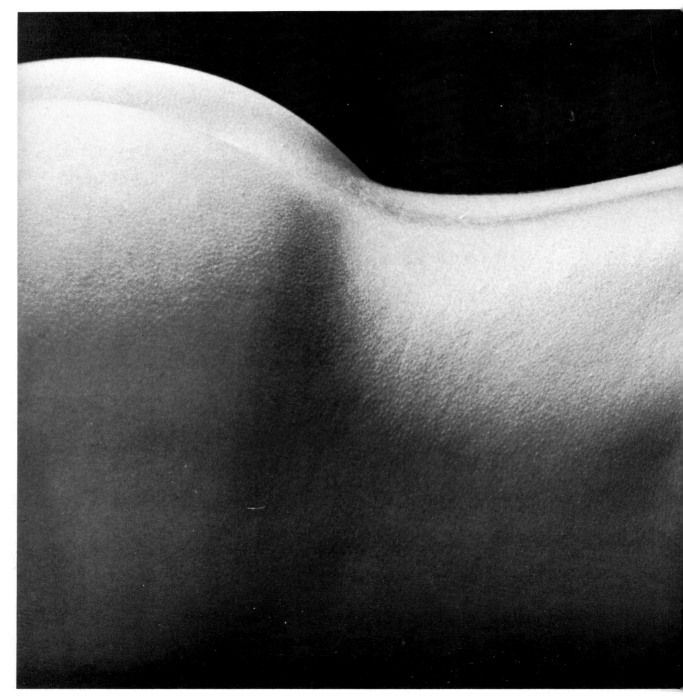

stoned

take a smooth
round rock
(size 4 to 5 lbs)
and place it for at
least 30 seconds
on different parts of
your body especially
those areas where
you feel tension
after take the rock away
and feel the effects

you can do the
experiment
with a partner
the receiver lies down
and is slapped
all over his back
or over the areas that
are to be sensitized
then after allowing
your partner time
to feel the effects
place the rocks
on different places

allow him time
to feel the effects
after 3 or 4
applications
with the rock
take it away and
allow your partner time
to feel the effects

in touch experience
a room

_____

go into a room
that is familiar
or new to you
close your eyes and
experience how your
hands feel
open your eyes
and clap your
hands together
at different rates
of speed
with various degrees of
intensity for 30 to 60
seconds
after put your hands
down
close your eyes and
feel what's happening
in your body
now raise your hands
to your waist line
and turn your palms
so that they face
one another
approximately 1 foot
apart
feel the energy flow
between them
after 20 seconds
open your eyes
and begin to touch
things in the room
walls rugs lamps objects
feel the different
shapes textures
after a while close
your eyes and continue
the exploration
after the experience
feel your hands
open your eyes
and see how the room
looks to you

who are you

_____

sit opposite
your partner and
for 5 minutes
one of you
repeats the question
who are you
the other person
must come up with
a different answer
each time
after 5 minutes
change places
when you have both
done the experiment
experience how you feel
and only then
should it be discussed

neck un tie

make 6 to 12
figure 8 movements
from the right base
of the neck to
the left base of the jaw
from the left base
of the jaw to the right
top of the head
from the right top
of the head to
the left top of the head
to the right base
of the jaw
from the right base
of the jaw
to the left base
of the neck
from the left base
of the neck
to the right base
of the neck
do the same number
of motions
in reverse order

eye rest

tear a napkin
in half and fold
each into a square
about 1½ x 1½ inches
dip them in some cold
water
and squeeze them
so they
are damp but
not dripping
lie on your back
close your eyes and
place one of the pads
over your left eye
after 30 seconds
remove it and
experience
how your left eye feels
compare it to
your right eye
now place a pad
over your right eye
after 30 seconds remove
the pad and experience
how you
and your eyes feel
then place the pads
over both eyes
at the same time
leave them there
as long as you wish
after open your eyes
look around and
be aware of
how things look
how you feel

feelings dance

when you're low
in a mood
don't just brood

move to your feelings
move with your feelings

get out
of your
inertia

DANCE

how you feel

x
static

be

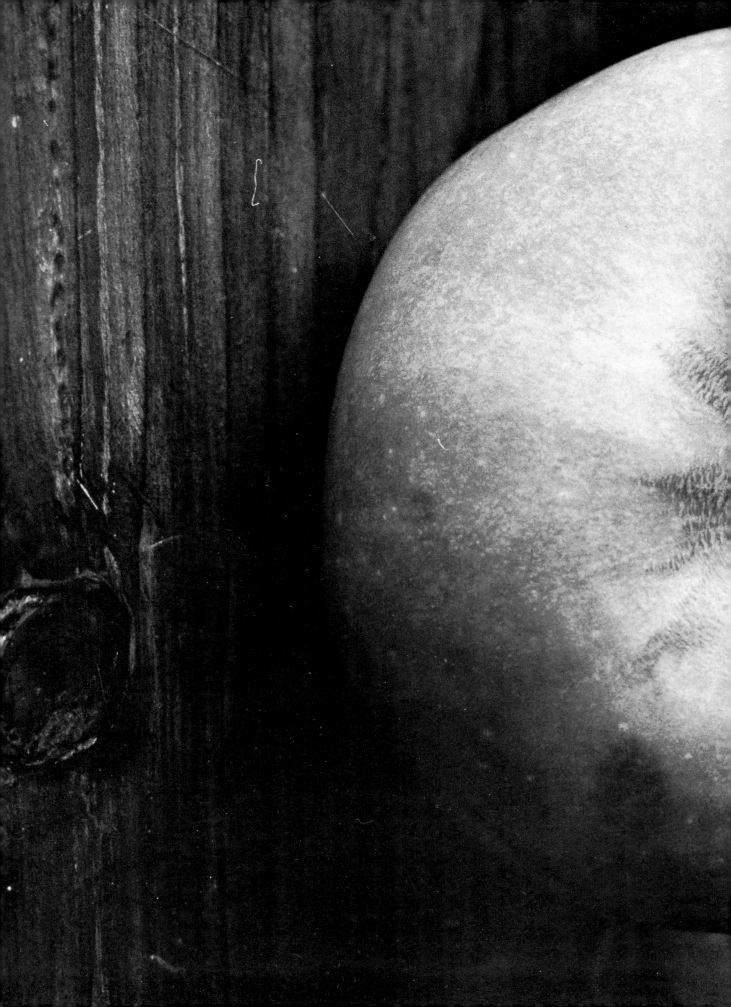

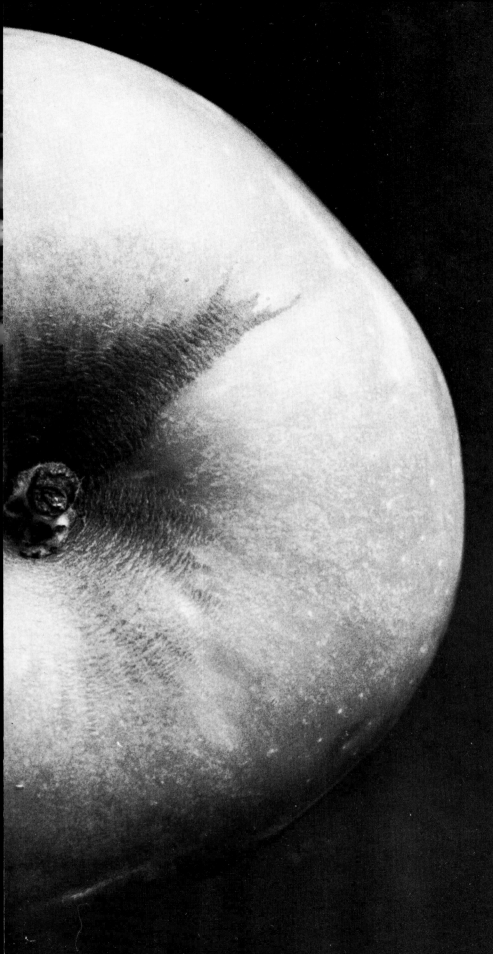

this apple

take an apple
(any kind of fruit)
sensitively wash
and polish it
see its shape
from many different
angles
feel its texture
with both hands
make sounds by tapping
or slapping the apple
feel its weight
smell the apple
toss it from one hand
to the other like a ball
close your eyes and
gently
rub the apple over your
entire face
sensitively rub it over
your lips and kiss
the apple
open your eyes
look at the apple again
then close your eyes
and take a bite
of the apple chewing
until you have
completely
liquified the bite
and then swallow it
open your eyes and
eat the rest of the apple
listening for the sounds
and see the changes
as the apple becomes
part of you

we all share
the same earth
water air
body of energy
but we most of the time
think/play
as if we were all
completely separate

every letter
on this page
is by itself
yet each exists
in relation to
words
sentences
paragraphs
individual letters
form a related whole

if one cell
in the physical body
is hurt
surrounding cells
are affected
if enough cells
are injured
then individual organs
or perhaps
the entire body
is destroyed

what do you
individually do
to the environment
we all share

how much physical
and mental
smog litter garbage
pollution hate
do you create

be aware

with care

every aware

**exist
dance**

celebrate

be
u
to
full

we are all
cells

in the great
bliss mind

consciousness
creation

participants

in the eternal
joy play

multi leveled

energy being

celebration

grow from an embryo

lying down
in an embryo position
experience how this
feels
slowly grow out
of this position
(take at least 1 minute)
until you are able
to crawl around the floor
for at least 1 minute
then slowly
make your way
up to all fours and
walk around this way
for a minute
in each of these
positions
see the world from that
point of view
next walk around
on your knees
and become aware
of this way of seeing
then slowly
with your eyes
closed stand up
experience what
standing
feels like with your
eyes closed then slowly
open your eyes and take
a look around you
go for a walk

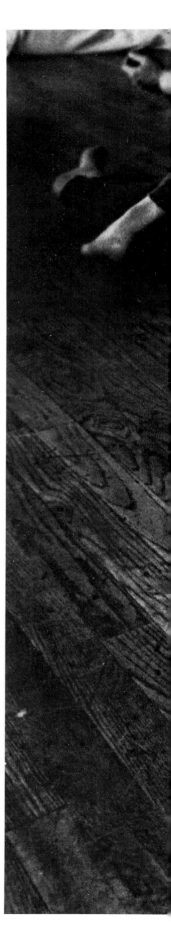

rebirth bath

give yourself time
to have a long
warm/hot bath
first soak
then with soap
slowly wash your body
next gently rub wet
table salt
all over you and
wash it off
now oil your entire body
and dry off

salt takes off the
dead skin of the surface
and your skin will be
like a new-born baby

silent coffee break

without talking/thinking
have a cup of coffee
see the cup
feel its shape
its weight
as you pour the coffee
see its color
listen to the sound
watch it as it is
being poured
experience the steam
the sugar
the cream
then sit down
and without rushing
non-verbally drink
your coffee

silent grace

without words
close your eyes and
chew savor
the full texture flavor
of the first bite
of food
at a meal
do not swallow
until that first
mouthful is
completely liquified
after open your eyes
and feast

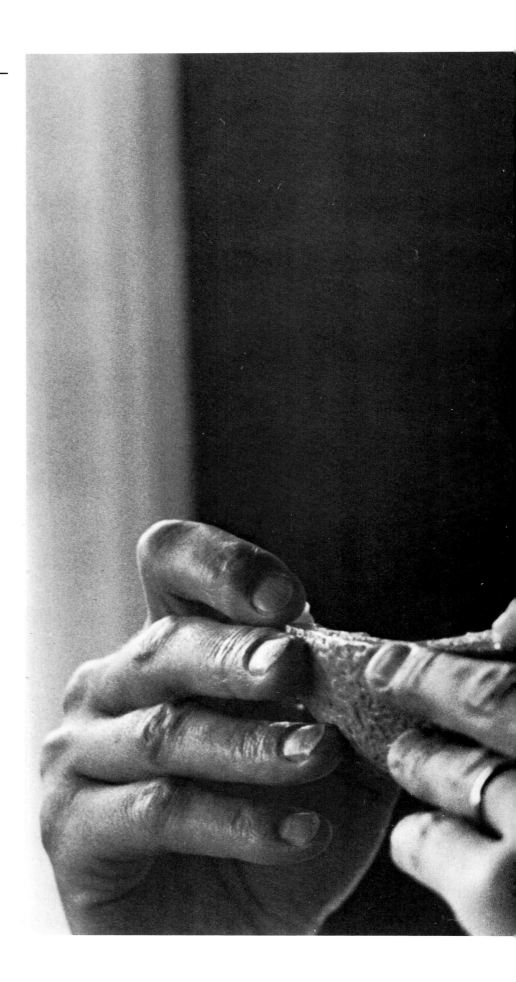

silent meal

---

without conversation
eat a meal
with someone else
or in a group

slowly

look
hear
taste
smell
feel

try eating with your
eyes closed
with or
without utensils

being together
_____

get together
with a group for
a given number of hours
without eating smoking
drinking sleeping
talking
or taking drugs
when the allotted time
is up
each of you goes
his own way
still in silence

you
dear god/man
put yourself
on the cross

feel yourself there

hung up

on destructive
thought patterns
negative action
excessive tension
ambition desire

you cut out
your heart feeling
stopping your energy
life excitement
and you can choose
to stay in agony or
pull the nails out with
insight/understanding
emotional release
constructive thinking
positive functioning

stop being so hard
on yourself

let go of your suffering
body tension

breathe deep

resurrect

your mind/body/spirit
in the joy full flowing
kingdom of heaven
is you here

hear
singing sounds
the sun
water air

be aware

right left
center

NOW

resurrection ceremony
_____

come off the cross
let go of your hang ups
and be reborn

one member
of a group of six
lies down
and thinks of a problem
or hang up
he would like to
get rid of
after giving him
some time
his partners cross
his legs at the ankles
and with their fists
as hammers
and their fingers
as nails they pin
their partner
to the ground
one partner
on each hand
one on the crossed
ankles
one partner
makes a crown
of thorns with his hands
the fifth partner puts his
hand and some pressure
on his pinned partner's
chest
the pressure on the
different part of the
body
is real but not
excessively hard
pain producing or
harmful
the person lying down
imagines he is in
great pain
and at a certain point
the pain becomes
unbearable
at that point he
lets go and
dies

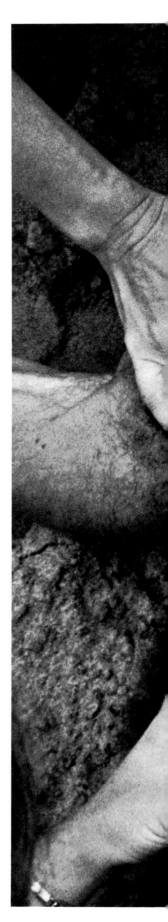

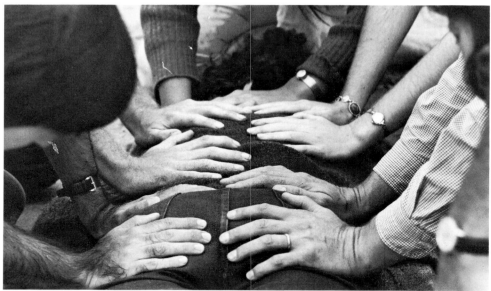

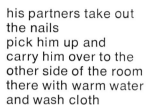

his partners take out
the nails
pick him up and
carry him over to the
other side of the room
there with warm water
and wash cloth

or just their hands
they wash his
hands face feet
then after a pause
they turn him over
and slap the back
of his body

after letting him absorb
this
with their hands
they caress his back
next after giving him
time
to digest the effects

they lay their hands
over his back
the hands remain there
for 30 seconds and then
they are slowly removed
the person who was
touched

stays down and
experiences
the effect of the touch
and then slowly gets up
and looks around
and sees who his
partners are

after a little time
another member
of the group
lies down
and the experience
is recreated

breaking of bread

take a loaf of fresh
unsliced bread
and pass it within
the group
so that each member
can touch feel smell it
then slowly with great
care
one person
breaks the bread
in half and passes
the two halves so that
each person can see
smell
and take a piece
of the bread
when that is done
everyone holds his
bread up
like drinking a toast
shuts his eyes
and slowly
eat/chews his
piece of bread
not swallowing until
it is completely
liquified

wine ceremony

sit in a circle
with a bottle of wine
and a chalice
in the center
one member of the
group
slowly pours the wine
into the chalice
while the other watch
its changing
shape color
listen hear its sounds
then the chalice
is passed around and
each member in turn
smells the wine
slowly touches
the wine to his lips
and then taste
drinks a sip of the wine

its divine

foot washing

---

after giving your partner
time to settle
slap his left foot
the whole foot
bottom top sides
then stop and give
him a moment to
feel the effects
of the slap
then slowly with
warm water feel
wash your partner's feet
first with soap and water
then with table salt
after sensitively drying
oil/massage
your partner's foot

after a pause
do the other foot

take your time

don't talk at all

allow plenty of space
between each step

rest

digest

work is worship
meditation
if you do it fully

with dedication

a sense of pride

care

holy

alive

aware

that the reward
is in the doing

action

for its own sake

not for the fruits

serve

serve
us

ALL

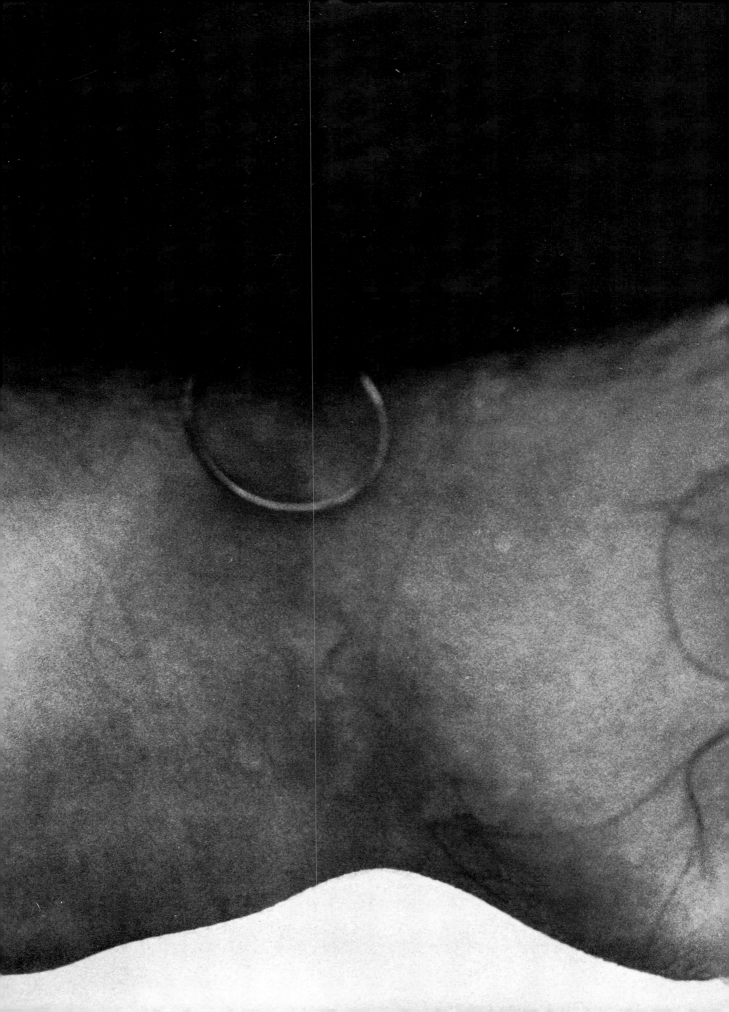

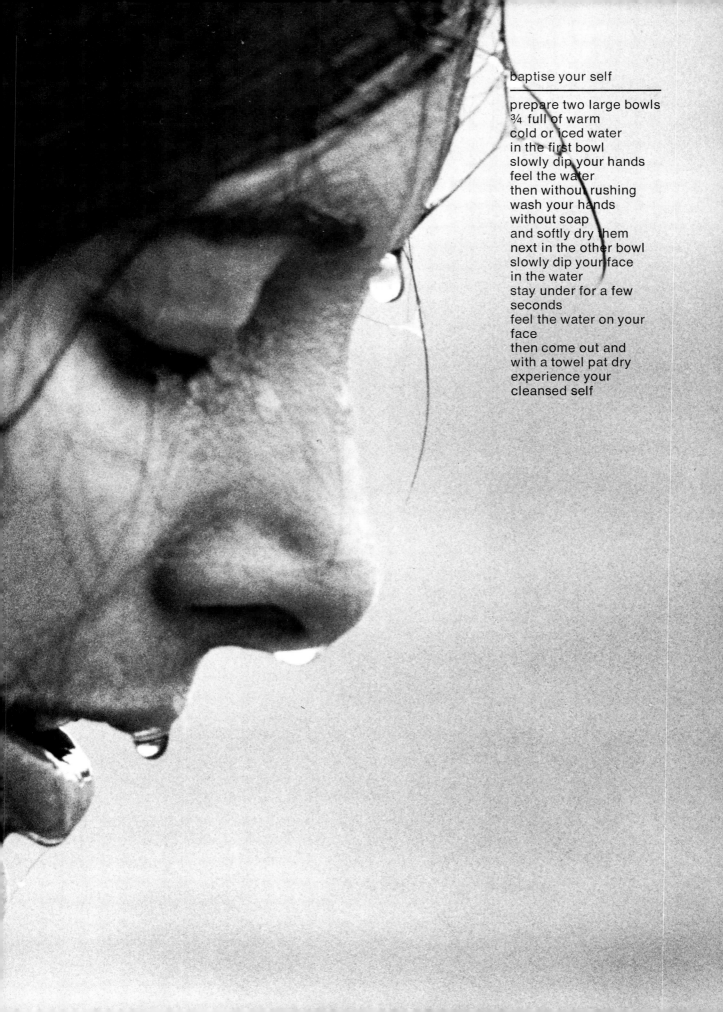

baptise your self

prepare two large bowls
¾ full of warm
cold or iced water
in the first bowl
slowly dip your hands
feel the water
then without rushing
wash your hands
without soap
and softly dry them
next in the other bowl
slowly dip your face
in the water
stay under for a few
seconds
feel the water on your
face
then come out and
with a towel pat dry
experience your
cleansed self

communion serving

as the group watches
slowly break
a loaf of bread
or a number of loaves
and pass a half
to each member
who in turn
looks at its shape
its firmness
its texture
smells the aroma
and then breaks off
a small piece for himself
and passes the loaf to his
neighbor
when everyone has a
piece of bread
everyone closes his
eyes and chews his
piece of bread
not swallowing
until he has completely
liquified it
then a large chalice
or a number of glasses
or cups
are brought in with
a bottle of wine
and as the group sits or
stands in a circle
and watches while the
bottle is uncorked and
the wine slowly poured
they listen to the sounds
see its color
its changing shape
then the containers are
passed to each person
who smells the wine
with his eyes closed
then brings the wine to
his lips
and without drinking
feels the wine
and then with his eyes
closed
he slowly
sips some wine
opens his eyes and
looks at
his neighbor as he
passes the cup
then after everyone has
had a sip allow the
group time
to digest the experience

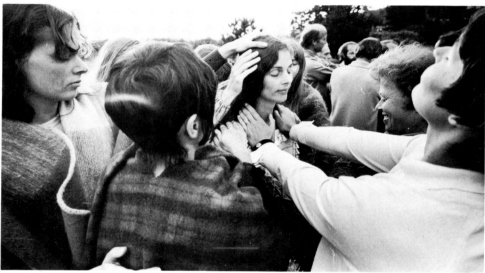

marriage ceremony

on one side of the room
all of the women
form a circle
around the bride
while on the other side
of the room
all of the men
surround the groom
the person in the center
of each circle closes
his eyes and is
slapped over his
entire body
by the surrounding
group
after slapping
the group gives the
center person
a chance to
digest the effects of the
slap and then the
entire group puts
their hands
somewhere on the body
of the person in the
center
as their hands remain
on the person
they send as much
loving energy
as possible
to the person
being touched
after 30 seconds or
more
all the people take
their hands away
the person in the
center without opening
his eyes feels
the effects
then the group comes
together
the two people
in the center
open their eyes
see one another
embrace and then
hand in hand
see all their friends
around them
at this point they may
be joined by a minister
or repeat their own vows
or have poetry read
exchange gifts or rings
then the group
joins them
in the middle of the
circle
with kisses
embraces
presents

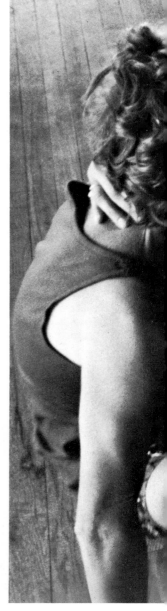

the laying on of hands
———————————————
the laying on of hands
may be done
by 2 people
3 people or with
a large group

in situations where
there is a smaller group
more applications
are made

the person who is
to receive lies
face down on the floor
or on a table
while he takes time
to get comfortable with
the floor and himself
his partner or partners
arrange themselves
so they
are in position to slap
and touch his
partner's back
then simultaneously
all of their hands
vigorously but gently
slap the entire back of
his body
back head to
bottom foot
after slowly and
gradually
let the slapping subside

the hands move away
and allow the passive
partner
a chance to experience
absorb the effects
during the time
this is done
the hands are busy

doing
finger energy flicks
do 60 to 100
next simultaneously
all of the hands
come to rest on
the back of
the lying down partner
if done by 1 or 2 people
the touch is repeated
with short pauses over
the entire back
when done
by a large group
all of the hands stay on
the physical body for

15 to 30 seconds
then slowly lift your
hands
¼ inch from the body
and hold them there
still for 10 seconds
then lower them again
on the body
as they make contact
with the body
the touchers see
a beam of white light
coming through the top
of their heads down
their necks shoulders
and arms and out their

hands and finger tips
the person
being touched
sees this white light
coming into his body
filling him with
harmonious energy
after 30 seconds
hands are again
lifted ¼ inch above the
physical body for
10 seconds
and then taken away
the partner lying down
stays down a while
to absorb

all of the energy effects
and then sits up and
sees
who his partners are

this touching process
may be repeated
a second time
or a new person
may lie down
and receive
the laying on
of hands

circle ceremony
——————————

each member of
a group
goes for a walk and
brings back something
from nature
a leaf rock acorn

flower or
personal belonging
and places it on
an altar or in
the middle of a circle
notice how individually
each person does it
sense each piece

and the changing
pattern
of the whole
and the shape of what
finally emerges
when everyone is done
stand up
put your arms around

one another and
move in a circle
seeing your composition
from different
points of view
then stop and slowly
raise your hand
into the air and

gradually
bring them down
to the side of your body
experience how you feel
let the composition
remain or
one by one remove
your contribution

DO NOT TALK DURING
THE EXPERIENCE

after bow
shake hands or
express yourself
in some non-verbal
way

peace embrace

both partners
close their eyes
and put their two hands
on each other's
shoulders
after letting their hands
rest there
for a few moments
without talking
they use their hands
to get to know
their partner's shoulders
(explore don't massage)
after 2 minutes
both partners stop
take a moment
to become aware
of themselves
and with their hands
still on their
partner's shoulders
they open their eyes
and see one another
after 15 seconds they
again
close their eyes
and pause to experience
after 15 seconds
one of the partners
takes one
of his hands away
from his partner's
shoulders
after a short pause
the other partner takes
one of his hands away
one by one
the two other hands
leave
after allowing time
to become aware of
themselves
the two partners
open their eyes and
embrace

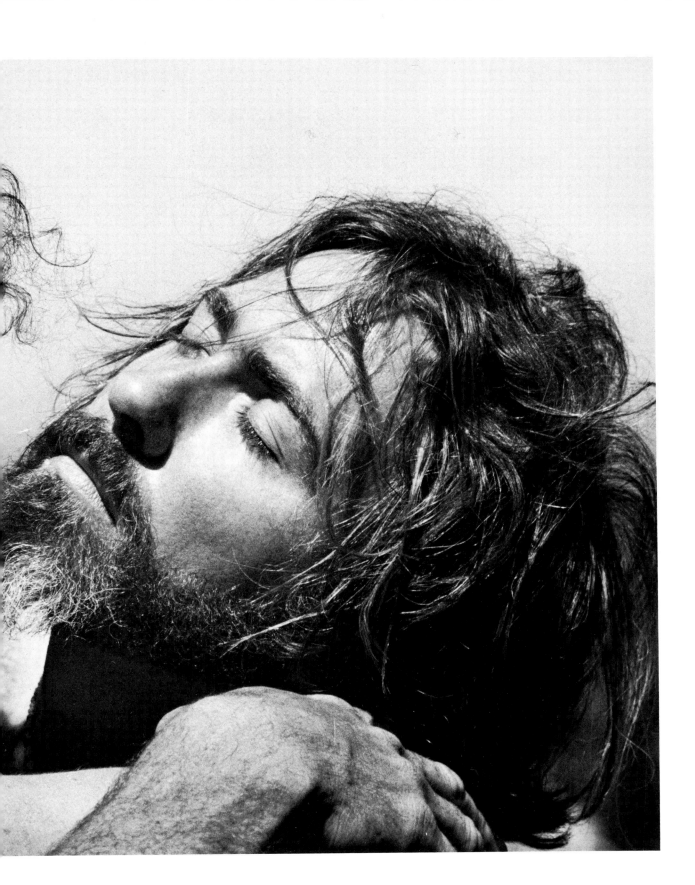

nomastay

rather than good bye
or good day
say: NOMASTAY
(in sanskrit:
I salute that in
you which is divine)

a reinforcing reminder
that within
each of us
there always dwells
that divine aspect

between

the two extremes

the genitals
nothing matters
screw everything

and

the head
up tightness
control everything

is

the new middle
the heart belly
experience awareness
love contact everything

head belly
heart genitals
mind body spirit

flowing
glowing

strong
soft

warm
cool

buddha
full

wise
fool

**glow
in peace**

eat

eat
chew
up

and
down

you
are

what
you
eat

think

do

slowly

taste

chew

digest

rest

and you

eating
less

will
be more

full

fully

satisfied

perls:

chewing is basic
aggression
de/struction
in the service
of self preservation
con/struction

if you do not
use it
to destroy food properly
it will create a
dis/sadist/faction
that will manifest itself
against you and others

periodically
or when you are angry
or frustrated
eat a carrot
an apple
or a hard piece
of bread
really bite into it
exaggerate your
chewing
experience the pleasure
taste texture
do not swallow until
you liquid/ate
the entire mass

we destroy
recre(ate)
and are
recre(ate)d

with your eyes closed
slowly
feed yourself
or be fed
an entire
meal

chew
feel

experience
a great deal

don't be a fanatic
but eat

natural
organic
unprocessed food
whenever possible

fresh
(not frozen)
fruits and
vegetables

a balanced amount
of fish or meat
to meet
your individual needs

keep the combinations
simple

AVOID
REFINED SUGAR

if you want to
make the
vegetarian scene
be sure to get
lots of protein
milk
eggs
cheese
nuts
soy beans

quality
food supplements
a good amount
of vitamin B C E
will help you to
continue to be
healthy

the law of karma

for every action
there is an equal
and opposite reaction

CAUSE AND EFFECT

if you eat
more food than
your body uses
you get fat

not enough sleep
you are tired

friendly people
have friends

it's simple

what ever you
think/do
in every way day
affects the
universe you

as you sow
so shall you
reap

think
fast

life
savor

don't eat

for one
two or three days

or one day
each week

just drink water

or

some kind of
fruit juice
(apple)

or

some kind of
vegetable juice
(carrot)

or

one kind of fruit
(watermelon)

or

one kind of vegetable
(zucchini)

rest work play
be extra aware all day
of your changing
mood moments
of clarity
great energy
elation

your physical system
refreshed
clean
lean
see/feel
what I mean

reflect

shut your
(infernal
internal)
trap

guilt is in the past
anxiety in the future
where is your mind

NOW

STOP

judging
what you
do
see

witness
experience
each
sensory
reality

everything is right
nothing is wrong
for things
are wrong
only as long
as they don't
belong
to what
we think
is right

but when
we long
for something
wrong
it becomes
all right

watch how your mind
goes to extremes

nobody loves me

we hate *everything*
you stand for

i *never* have any fun

nothing ever turns out
right

observe
the temporary
one sideness
of opposites

i hate you

i love you

i need you

who needs you

recognize and modify
your statements
in perspective

see the whole totality
of your deceptive
verbal reality

some people suffer

just for the hell
of it

the kingdom
of heaven
and hell
is with/in
you

sit or lie back
take your time
and as vividly
as possible
feel remember
some of the
following:

remember what it feels
like to relax
remember what it feels
like to lie in the sun
remember how it feels
to get out of fresh water
remember the taste of
your favorite beverage
remember your
favorite food
remember what it feels
like to be loved
remember the feeling of
a cool refreshing breeze
remember a beautiful
scene
remember doing some-
thing for someone
remember being happy
remember how it feels
after a good night sleep
remember how it feels
after washing your face
remember a lovely
aroma
remember your favorite
piece of music
remember someone you
loved to touch
remember how things
look by candle light
remember a pleasant
day at the beach
remember how ice
cream tasted as a kid
remember a fresh sheet
and a warm bed
remember how good it
feels to urinate
after a long wait
remember the movies as
a kid
remember a sound of a
stream
remember how soft a
flower feels
remember your best
high
remember a teacher you
liked
remember a taste of a
hot dog

remember your best
sexual experience
remember a great meal
remember what it feels
like to laugh
remember being
at peace
remember fresh air
remember soft hair
remember a great kiss
remember someone
who makes you happy

dare
challenge

have a
contact
encounter
confrontation

with each

person
belief
activity

now new

experience

your self

every
moment

situation

if you're fully in
each situation
meeting
moment

you won't have to
possess

ANY ONE

find
out
what
you
want

ASK DIRECTLY
FOR WHAT
YOU WANT

chances are it
will be given
to you
if not
you can find
some other
situation/person
who will

take a chance
on getting slapped
you might
get kissed

learn to trust your self

don't compare yourself
with anyone else

be
beyond
compare

become aware
of your fears
your expectations
how you make them
happen

great expectation
great disappointment

little expectation
little disappointment

no expectation
no disappointment

listen
to your voice

is it small
disembodied
monotonous
whining
complaining
saccharine
unctuous
straining

feel each word
in connection
with your body

use your hands

don't depress yourself
express yourself

if you are
in conflict
with in your self
have the
different parts
talk out loud
to one another

listen
to what they
have to say
to each other

feel find out
what they/you
really want
to do

some people are
gloomcasters
their only happiness
is making everybody
unhappy

others are like
vampires out to drain
all your energy

some think sharing
their problems
is the magic road
to instant intimacy

speak up

don't be sucked in

if you let
everyone dump
their load
problems
on you
you will be

d
o
w
n

i
n

t
h
e

d
u
m
p
s

FEEL

the difference between

i should
and
i want to

i can't
and
i won't

i must
and
i will

i need
and
i want

there may be
lots of things
you want
there are
very few things
that you
really need

be aware
of your thoughts
fantasies all day
when you don't
like the direction
they are taking
change them
in a positive way

in your mind's eye
see things
turning out
coming to pass
the way you
want them to

pictures
and feelings
speak to your
unconscious
better than words

for 15 minutes
each day
picture/feel
what you want
the way you want
your life to be
see it as vividly
with as much detail
as possible
feel experience see
what you want
as if it has
already happened

REMEMBER

you are the ring master

your thoughts/emotions
your friends/demons
energy

what are your thoughts

how do you create
your pleasure/pain life

each/every thought
is a brick
in the continuous
building
of your existence

what kind of
positive/negative
material (thoughts)
are your thought bricks
composed of

watch your thinking
either you play
with your mind
or your mind plays with
you

words
thoughts
images
dreams
are all real
to your
consciousness

your word is law
to this accepting servant

be aware
it will do what you
knowingly or
unknowingly
ask/tell it to

so stop and
THINK

change your thinking
for a change

dreams are
direct messages
from your unconscious
which uses symbols
pictures that
say more than words

you are all
of the aspects
of your dream

feelings
people
objects

it's an endless task
to analyze them
or try to figure out
what they mean

rather see your dream
as a play

act it out

have each
of the characters
objects feelings
introduce themselves

i am a chair
i don't go anywhere
everybody sits on me

i am anger
i am red
you never let me
express myself
i wish you were dead

then have them talk
confront one another
tell each other
what their feelings are
toward the world and
one another
work it out till they
understand each other

so that they/you
can resolve your
inner differences

and become

wholly one

be your own doctor

be patient
with yourself

patience
if given a chance
can enhance
the soul's dance
to advance

don't overstand

UNDERSTAND
YOURSELF

become your
own friend

think well
of yourself

don't put
yourself down

reinforce
rather than
divorce
yourself

**be
no
bull**

breathe

**stop
holding
your
breadth**

respiration is
elation

cleansing

exhalation

vitality
energy
inspiration

fear
control is
with holding

repression
suppression
depression

breathing
is an automatic
self regulating process
which works perfectly
unless you habitually
inhibit misdirect
inner fear

a bridge between
the conscious
and unconscious mind

breathing patterns
can create
well being or
hell being

a psychophysical
meditation
breathing exercises
properly done
affect every
transaction
interaction

so breathe
chant
shout

let
in
out

vacuum cleaner
_____

take a quick gasp
of air into your throat
all you can get in
through your mouth
in one gasp
hold it and experience
the pressure it causes
in your neck
now open your lips
and slowly let
the air out
when you think
you have
exhaled completely
bend forward
at the waist
and actually finish
the exhalation
then allow a fresh
new breath of air
to come in
don't force/breathe it
let it happen

if you only half breathe
you never really
clear your lungs
which remain half full
of CO_2 residue
to get a whole new
supply in
you have to rid yourself
of the old air

be empty
open to the new

tranquil/i's	air in out	complete breath	his/sing breath

tranquil/i's

3 times a day
morning
evening
afternoon
sit down and
breathe in
at a count of 8
as you bring the air
in through your mouth
let your stomach
come out
as you breathe out
through your nostrils
at the count of 8
your stomach comes in

repeat 15 times
at each sitting

watch how
babies
animals
belly
breathe
free

air in out

through your mouth
take in a full breath of
air
as you take it in
feel/see this fresh air
coming into your feet
and toes
spreading over this
entire area
as you exhale see/feel
all of the old air
waste going out
through your nose
do this procedure
over your entire body
or in any specialized
areas of tension
you may do up to 3 to 5
breaths
in any one place
after experience
the area you have
worked on
your body
your being

complete breath

sit on the edge
of a chair
with your back straight
exhale completely
take in air in your mouth
at the count of 12
(take one second for
each count)
as you take in
4 counts of air
let your stomach come
out
then take in 4 more
counts of air
as your chest raises up
finally raise
your shoulders
taking in air for
4 more counts
hold the air in
your shoulders up
for 4 counts
your hands rest
on your knees
then slowly
start to exhale
through your nostrils
slowly lower your
shoulders
in 4 counts
your chest in 4 counts
your stomach
in 4 counts
when you return to
the starting position
let no air in for 4 counts
and start again

repeat this exercise
5 to 10 times

air is taken in
through the mouth
and let out through
the nostrils
in a continuous flowing
motion

it is important
to space/regulate
the amount of air
so that your lungs
are not full or empty
before you reach
the count of 12

his/sing breath

with your lips open
your teeth together
and your tongue
held in suspension
suck in air
through your mouth
while exhaling
a hissing sound is made
and your attention
is placed on the cool
feeling on your tongue
hold the air in
as long as you are
comfortable
release the air
slowly out your nose

rhythmic breath

breathe in
at the count of 3
hold your breath
while concentrating
between the eyebrows
for a count of 12
let the air out
at a count of 6

repeat this exercise
10 to 15 times

change the count
if you desire
as long as you
keep the ratio
of 1-4-2

cooling breath

the tongue protrudes
between your lips
the mouth is half open
making a hissing sound
as the air is brought in
bring in your tongue
and close your mouth
hold the air in
as long as you
are comfortable
exhale through
the nose

as the air enters
imagine light and
energy
coming in

as you exhale
see waste and fatigue
leave

concentrate so that
it is not just
a mechanical
physical exercise
but a meditation

calm/in breath

place the tip
of the index and
middle finger
of your right hand
on your forehead
just above the eyebrows
so that the thumb
can press against and
close the right nostril
and the ring and little
finger can press and
close the left nostril

to start
place your fingers
in the above position
and then open
the left nostril
and let all of the air out
close the left nostril
and hold the air out
for a count of 4
now open the left nostril
and take in air
for a count of 8
close the left nostril
again
concentrate on
the middle of your
forehead
and count to 4

then open
the right nostril
and let air out for
the count of 8
close the right nostril
for a count of 4
then reverse the process
open the right nostril
for a count of 8
close the right nostril
for a count of 4
open the left nostril
for a count of 8
close both nostrils
for a count of 4
open the left nostril
for a count of 8
and start the cycle again

let the air in and out
in a steady even flow

count slowly
each count is 1 second

repeat this cycle
5 to 10 times

chanting
is a great way
to start or end
or enhance your day

it's a sound way
to clear your lungs
of old residual air so
that a fresh supply
of life energy
can enter there

creating a better
oxygen carbon dioxide
balance

chanting vibrations
also have a toning
relaxing effect
on the personality
nerves muscles and
organs
of the entire organism

alone
aloud

with yourself
with others
refresh
regenerate

be

in

chanting

vibrating vowels

close your eyes
and take a moment
to feel yourself
how your breathing is
then exhale completely
take a deep breath
as you release the air
make the high pitched
sound EEEeeeeee
concentrate on feeling
the vibration
in the center of your
head
let the sound/air out
until the breath
is finished
allow for a couple of
natural breaths before
repeating the sound
1 or 2 times more or
moving on to the next
sound AAAaaaaaa
(pronounce as in play)
concentrate the
vibration
in your throat
either repeat this sound
or move on to the next
vowel Aaahhh
which you focus
in the chest
now move to the belly
and make the sound
OooMmm
this sound is divided
into 2 syllables
the Oohh consists of the
first half of the breath
while the Mmmmmm
utilizes the second half
the final sound is
UUUuuu
(pronounce as in true)
concentrate the
vibration
in the region of the hips
after keep your eyes
closed
and experience
how you feel

in a word

take one word
that has a lot
of meaning for you
like LOVE
or the name
of a person who
you feel is an
inspiration like
JESUS or BUDDHA
close your eyes and
repeat this word
or name over and over
for 5 to 15 minutes
after keep your eyes
closed
and experience
how you feel

your sound

after doing
one of the other chants
by yourself or
with a group
get involved with
making your own sound
allow hear
whatever sound or
series of different
sounds
wants to emerge
if you are with a group
stand in a circle
hands on
each others' shoulders
and harmonize blend
individual sounds
with one another
high and low
soft loud slow

let it
flow

om

OM is the first sound
the total sound
the collective sound
of the universe

close your eyes
take a deep breath
as you let the air out
make the sound Ooohhh
when you have let half
your breath out
make the
vibrating sound
MMMmmm
when that breath is over
allow yourself time
for a couple of natural
breaths before
repeating the chant
5 or more times
after keep your eyes
closed
and experience
your feelings

if done in a group
put your arms around
one anothers shoulders
and stand in a circle
at different times
alternate and blend
male and female voices

shanty means peace

this chant
is to be sung
specifically for peace

repeat over and
over again

om
shanty
om
shanty

om
shanty
om

life
is

breath
taking

and
giving

energize

**energys
us**

all   life loves

the world   shifting

you are   expanding
                             desire
is energy
                             changing
different
degrees   creating
amounts   patterns
of speed
                             diversity
density
intensity   structure

in very/us   position
forms
                             one
atoms   bright
molecules
                             unity
solid   light
liquid
gas   energy
jewels   consciousness

sound   composition
sensing
feeling
thought
muscles
in space

mind/body
generator
degenerator
regenerator

action

reaction

electricity
chemistry

on the plane
of the earth
air
water
fire

stimyoumeelation

the group walks around
interweaving with
one another
first at normal speed
next moving through
traffic
very fast and then slowly
after a time they begin
to slap each others' right
hand as they pass
next they slap
each others'
left hand and then
both hands
simultaneously
after they walk around
experiencing how
their hands feel
then they move around
trying to touch
each other
without being touched
after a while they do
the touching
in slow motion
then they put their
hands down
and walk around letting
their breathing return
to normal
and experiencing
how they feel

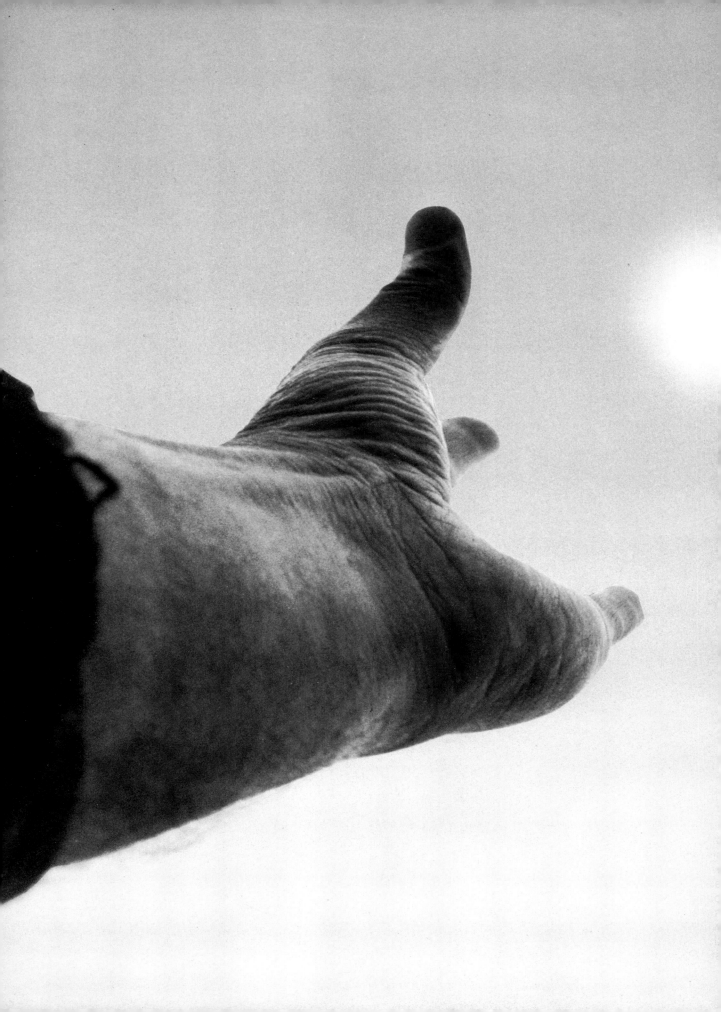

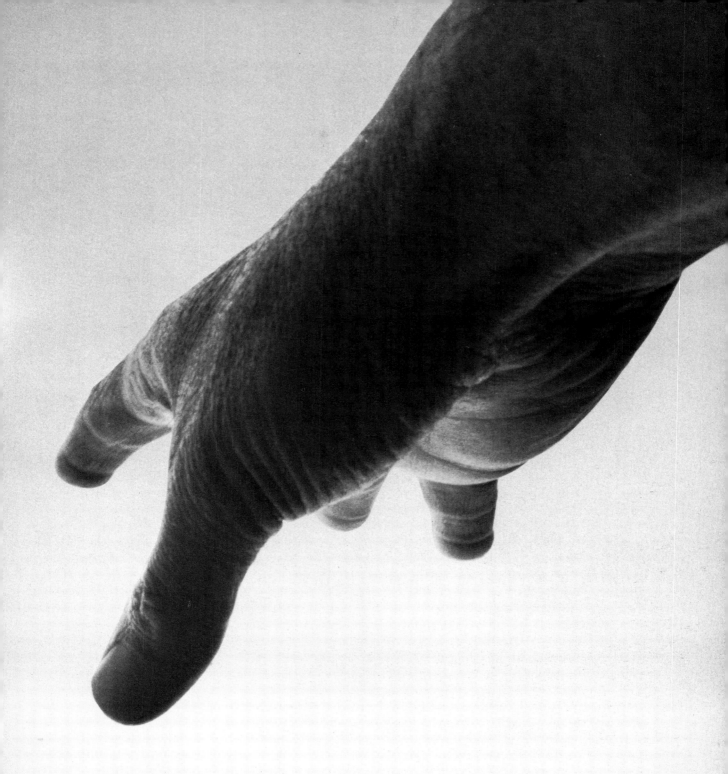

finger energy flicks
_____

hold both arms
straight out
shoulder high
with your right palm up
and your left
palm down
make a fist
with both hands and
then quickly open
stretch

and close hands
back to a fist
continue this action
without pause
or hesitation 10 times
now turn the right
palm down
and left palm up
repeat the open/close
hand action
10 more times
every time

you do 10 flicks
alternate the
right/left palms
up and down
start with 60 to 100
and work up to 200
(in the beginning
your hand/fingers will
become fatigued
until you get used
to this motion)
after close your eyes

and experience the
energy
in your hands and arms
let it flow
into the rest of
your body

energy at your
finger tips
hands
feeling
healing

lighting up

you are an energy field
surrounded by a greater
energy field

first do the
finger energy flicks
then close your eyes
and feel the effects
moving through you
next see a white light
of energy
beaming into the top
of your head
and filling your being
with harmony
and vitality
after 3 minutes
see an orchid colored
light streaming from
your solar plexus
and moving out
towards the world

this meditation is
done for 10 minutes

energy heal thyself

lie on your back
on the floor or
on a bed
close your eyes and
keep them closed
during this entire
experiment
after allowing time
to settle
place both your hands
on the area of your
solar plexus
around the area of
the navel
both palms rest flat
and the fingers
on one hand do not
overlap or touch
the other
become aware of the
breathing/movement
that is going on there
then after 1 minute
half curl your fingers
so that just
your finger tips
rest on your stomach
now picture a white light
of energy
coming from
this area and
as you breathe in
at a count of 7
see this white light
coming into
your finger tips
hold it there
as you take
your hands away
and place them
on any area
of your body that you
wish to heal energize
or relieve of pain
as you exhale
just your finger tips
touch the area at a
count of 7
see the white light come
out of your finger tips
and into that area
that is being worked on
repeat this procedure
6 to 12 times
after experience how
you
feel

this process may be
repeated
2 or 3 times a day

most of this experiment
may be done
in a sitting position
and energy can be
transferred to others
as well

after bringing the
light energy
into your fingers
place them on your
friends body and as
you exhale
see the white light
enter his body
the person receiving
see the light come
into his body
fill him with
harmonious healing
energy

light energy flowing
———————————————

the receiving person
lies down on his back
and closes his eyes
the two partners
who are going to do
the touching
take their places at
the head and feet
of the person to be
touched
after giving the lying
down person enough
time to settle
the foot partner
bends down and
gently but firmly
takes hold
of his partner's
ankles holding them
without motion
after approximately
30 seconds
he takes his hands away
from the ankles
and the head partner
gently/firmly puts his
hands
on the side
of his partner's head
after approximately
30 seconds
of motionless contact
he takes his hands away
and the two standing
partners change places
and without hurrying
they simultaneously
take hold of the head
and the ankles or their
partner on the floor
close their eyes and
see a white light
coming into the top
of their heads
this energy light
moves down
their shoulders
and arms
out their hands and
into the person
on the floor

the receiving partner
while lying on his back
sees the light coming
into his head and feet
filling his body with
warmth and harmony
after 1 minute
the 2 partners
take their hands away
and the partner lying
down is allowed
time to absorb the
effects

the treatment may
be repeated
2 or 3 times

after the lying down
partner opens his eyes
and sees who his
partners
are

change places

calming clock wise circles

the person
to receive lies
down on his back
and closes his eyes
after giving yourself
and your partner
a few moments
to quiet down place
the palm of your hand
½ inch away from
your partner's
solar plexus
let it remain still
for 15 seconds
and then slowly
make 9 to 15
clock wise circles
about 6 inches in
diameter
over the area
after the circles
let your hand remain
still over the area
for 15 to 30 seconds
before taking
your hand away
after allow
your partner to
rest and digest the
experience

this experiment
helps create
a quiet calmness
and soothe disturbance

especially
recommended
for pregnant women

you can even make
these circles over
your own center

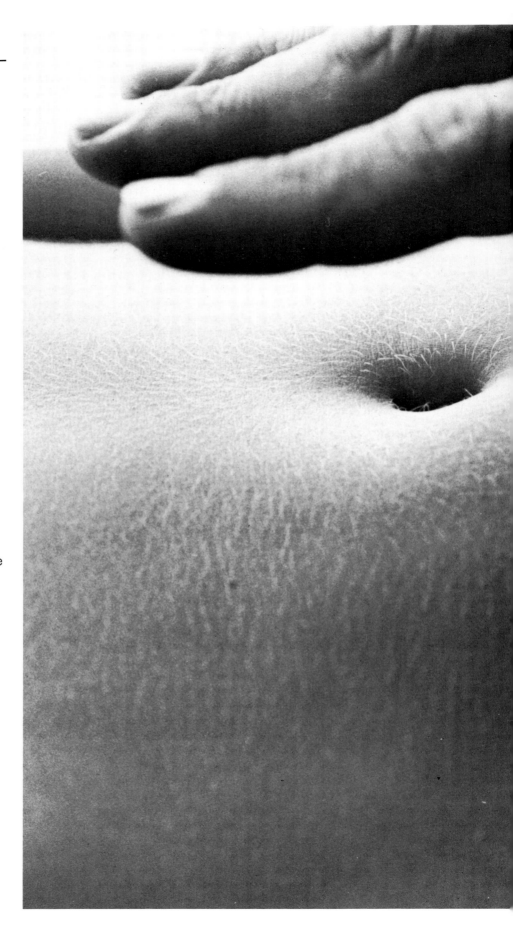

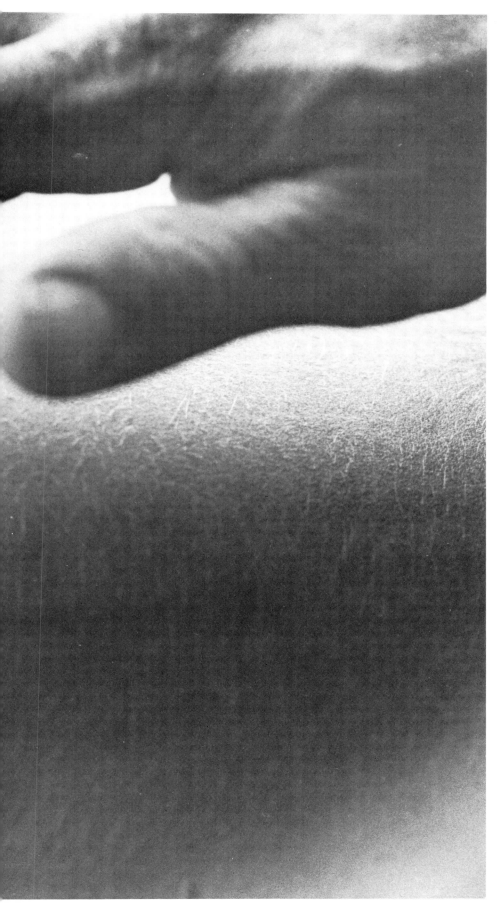

your bright light

sit straight
and close your eyes
see a bright white light
between your shoulder
blades
bring this stream of light
into your left shoulder
arm forearm hand
and let it flow
out your fingers
again focus between
your shoulder blades
and send the white light
down your torso
through your left hip
thigh calf and
out your left foot
again return to the light
between your shoulder
blades
this time see the beam
fill your chest stomach
across the pelvic floor
and up each of the
vertebrae
up your spine
bring the light
up over the top of
your head
down your face and
neck
and back to between
your shoulder blades
experience the light
there
and how you feel

energy field day
_____

have each member of a
group
move to the opposite
side of the room
in many different ways
have the group notice
how differently
people move

1. walk
2. walk as fast as you
   can
3. skip
4. hop
5. run
6. run waving your
   hands
7. run and shout as loud
   as you can

have each member of
the group
take partners
and each couple
moves to the opposite
end of the room
the group observes
partners may be
switched after
each experience

1. walk together
2. walk fast together
3. skip together
4. hop together
5. run together
6. figure out an unusual way to move across the room together

have 2 people on opposite ends of the room move toward each other/the center of the room while the rest of the group watches

1. meet and experience what happens
2. try to touch the other persons before they touch you
3. do a dance together

a mad king
lived in the cellar
of his castle
and in spite
of everything
his wise ministers
told him
about the
golden throne room
and the unlimited
possibilities
up stairs
the king continued to
live
down there

sexual energy
is your treasure

which can be channeled
into spiritual growth
creativity
reproduction
pleasure

it is your primary source
life force self

which can be spent
saved
squandered

experience the value
of periodic celibacy
doing without
sexual intercourse
or orgasm
for 3 to 6 weeks

concentrate on the
subtle vigor joy
you gain rather than
think about the
momentary pleasure
you are giving up

your greater
mental agility

creative
ability

emotional
stability

energy peaks

speaks
for itself

energy

must be used

positively
constructively

or it will
be abused

negatively
destructively

expressed
in creative functioning
elation

or

depressed
into anger anxiety
frustration

tension is energy
that wants to be

love

shared

spent

allowed to
flow free

**god
un
dam
me**

sleep

shut i

trust your own body

no/body else
can tell you
how much sleep
you need

if you wake
early or
in the middle
of the night
don't fight
to get back
to sleep

become aware
of what's going on
what it's trying
to tell you

use the energy
to meditate
take a bath or shower
read write
or clean the house

it's true
insomnia is a
problem
but it's certainly
nothing to lose
any sleep over

to sleep

get undressed
read for rest
and when you're ready
to sleep close your eyes
experience
what your breathing
is like
after about 30 seconds
in your mind's eye
one by one *feel*
with your consciousness
the different areas
of bones in your body
toes
feet
lower legs
knees
thighs
hips
vertebral column
ribs
collar bone
jaw
skull

experience your organs
genitals
intestine
stomach
heart
lungs
tongue
eyes

be aware of each set
of muscles
toes
feet
calves
thighs
anus
belly
back
chest
arms
forearms
hands
fingers
shoulders
neck
mouth
face
scalp

let yourself go
to sleep

peace

**yourself
together**

meditate

real
eyes
don't
conceptual
lies

stop

your wandering

attention

there is an inner
as well as
an outer life
and a need
to balance
interlink the two

your
prime
merry
process

inner/outer
flowing energy
harmony you

the mind is like
a drunken monkey
that has just been
bitten by a scorpion

an undisciplined child
that you have let
run wild

slowly with practice
patience
you can teach this child
how to pin point
think/act
the way you
want/will it to

through

channeled attention

concentration

awareness

MEDITATION:

that point at which
subject and object
being and experience
fuseintoone

the direct experience
sensation
innovation
of each/every situation
without bias
or indoctrination

wide

open

there are many
kinds forms
of meditation
as there are
various types
of people
unless you have
personal contact
with a master
it is desirable
to try a number of
different varieties
until you find
the kind
that fits your mind
sits best with you

it is desirable
to meditate
at a certain time
each day
in the same quiet
place way
if this is not possible
do your best
whenever you can

sit in a chair
with both feet flat
on the floor or
in a crossed legged
position on the floor

your neck and back
need to be straight
but not stiff

for inner meditation
your eyes are
shut or lowered
to avoid distraction

start by taking
a deep breath
becoming aware
of your breathing
or practice taking
your consciousness
through your body
or both of these

do not meditate
lying down unless
you are too weak
to do it
any other way

usually
you will find
the mind
continually leaving
the moment
the subject you
are to keep
your attention on
continuously
bring it back

REMEMBER

many things
that start off easily
end in misery
meditation
starts with difficulty
and ends in pleasure
bliss harmony

NOW

meditation can be
sitting quiet inwardly
or in every/any
work
movement
sensory play
activity

who am i
_____

close your eyes
and think/realize
you are not your name
or your roles
you are not your body
emotions sensations
goals
for they are
always changing
never the same
you are not your mind
thoughts are
another game
then
who am i
continue to question

keep asking
YOURSELF

every breath counts

for 10 to 15 minutes
or longer
fix your attention
on your breathing
and with out
controlling
or interfering
with it in any way
count each inhalation
of breath from
1 to 10 then
start your count
over again
each time your mind
wanders or you lose
count start counting
over again

be aware of
the pauses
between the inhalation
and the exhalation
allow the pause to be
as long as it
wants to be

count each exhalation
for a variation

empty headed

sit in a chair
or on the floor
close your eyes and
make your mind a blank
or picture a blank
screen
in your mind's eye
now for 5 to 15 minutes
concentrate on keeping
your mind free
of thoughts and images
except for the blank
screen
each time you catch
yourself think/dreaming
clear your head
and bring it back
to emptiness

candle meditation

sit in a chair
or on the floor
place a lighted candle
3 feet from you
and for 2 minutes
look directly into
the flame
if your mind wanders
bring it back
to the flame
see its height
watch it dancing
movement
see all of the colors
within the flame
when the 2 minutes
are over
close your eyes
and place the palms
of your hands over
your eyes
and see the after image
of the flame
in your mind's eye
concentrate on
that image
if it disappears
or your mind wanders
bring it back
after 2 minutes
open your eyes
and repeat
this sequence
1 or 2 more times

candle
light
delicate
dancing

without emotion
expecting no reward

merely
totally

being

defecation meditation

fix your attention
on what you are doing
and just sit
and wait
don't make anything
happen
just be

patiently

open

allowing
sensation
feeling

become aware
of how
your mind wanders
of your attitudes
the way you go
about this basic function

if you lose
your patience
become nervous
need to rush
force finish
get it over with
be conscious
accept how you are
only then will you
in time
if you desire
gradually be
able to change

symbols of integration

sit down and
close your eyes and
for 5 minutes draw
with blue light
in your mind's eye
a clockwise circle
with a dot in the center
after each dot
make another circle

next make a triangle
in your mind's eye
with blue light
it is important
to draw the symbol
in the following order
right bottom to right top
right top to left bottom
left bottom
to right bottom
draw a continuous
series of triangles
for 5 minutes

finally make
symmetrical
crosses with blue light
it is important to draw
the crosses
in the following order
come from the bottom
to the top
from the left side
to the right side
this is done in a
continuous series of
crosses

total time
is 15 minutes

this meditation must
be done every day
for at least 3 months

if you have difficulty
visualizing
draw the symbols
on your left palm
with your right
index finger

a rose opening

lie in a comfortable
place or sit in a chair
close your eyes
and see in
your mind's eye
a beautiful
closed rose bud
become that rose bud
experience how you feel
your shape
your size
your color
your stem
your leaves
your connection with
the ground
the sun is
shining on you
feel the warmth
of the sun
as you begin to bloom
gentle raindrops
fall on you
as you continue to
open wider
feel yourself
surrounded by
caressing air
which is always there
gently embracing you
as you open still more
a warm soft wind
gently flows through you
asking you
to blossom to
birds singing songs
and the sounds of
nature
ask you to expand as
the warm sun continues
to shine
filling you with
warm glowing energy
until you are
all the way open
in full bloom

take at least 5 minutes
to do this experiment

after experience
yourself

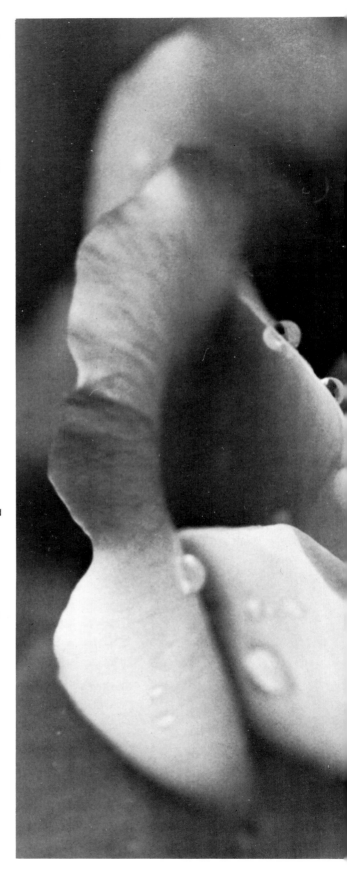

sensory meditation
is not
something you just do
sometimes
at seminars
in certain situations
special moments
but an integral part
of each/every rich
moment LIFE

become aware
of how you move
breathe sense
experience your life

at times
become conscious
of your acts
do them in slow motion

watch the ocean
though it sometimes
moves fast
it never rushes

find out how your body
in each situation
wants to act/be
harmoniously

now and then
close your eyes
experience in silence
allow yourself to be
more sensitive
aware that
all being
eating
drinking
sensing
non/thinking

is meditation

our loss of
harmony/balance
with nature
reflects the lack
of communication
and understanding
with/in

our culture education
over stress
the mind
symbolic functioning
ignoring imagination
sensation intuition
feeling

we over eat
think
hurry
do
screw
our energy away
our selves up

we pollute the body
self abuse
the excessive use
of drugs
tobacco
alcohol
processed food

we value status
symbolic wealth
rather than health
friendship
peace

we cease to live
in the present
and fantasies
in the goal anxiety
of the future
the glory guilt
of the past

misuse our mind/bodies
create chronic tension
isolation
hold our breath
worry ourselves to death

ecology
is life conservation
proper breathing
body care
relaxation
elimination
contemplation

existence balancing

activity
food
study
play
rest

the best of
east and west

inner and outer
mind body spirit

meditation
thought
and deed

withdrawal and
participation

unity and
individuation

realization

growing
consciousness

understanding

integration

your
inner
outer

rhythm
balance
cycle

concentration
absorbation
meditation

taking in

energy
wisdom

to restore

digestion
for more

utilization

creative
worldly
functioning

to out pour

foe
kiss

love

u
is
half
of
us

physical love
not sex

is worship

the sacred
renewing reunion
of god and goddess
male and female
yin and yang
duality of the universe

love is not
something you make

but a sensitive
feeling experience
that you allow

love
not two
grab push
force squeeze
restrict power
hinder devour

but two open
kiss touch
caress flow
sensitive care
tender grow

love
two know
to come
together

it's not a matter
of what you do
but how
and with who

look
you've
never seen
me before

it's all in
your imagination

accept right now
you in my arms
alive
NOW

an infinity
to foreplay
with one another

kiss much
touch much
feel much
much
warming to each other

take your timelessness

opening

so that entrance
is soft firm
and easy

letting
experience
union
long
last

let the process
go slow
or be with
no movement

don't rush (hurry)
there's no place
to go

just know
this oneness
moment

no goal
no need to climax

just water falling
in the endless stream
of life

sharing loving energy
closeness
in kiss caress
touch

your
my
high
ness

describe your partner

sit in a chair
or on the floor
knee to knee
and for 3 to 5 minutes
look at your partner
and describe
what you are seeing
start each sentence with
i see
after reverse roles
for the same
amount of time

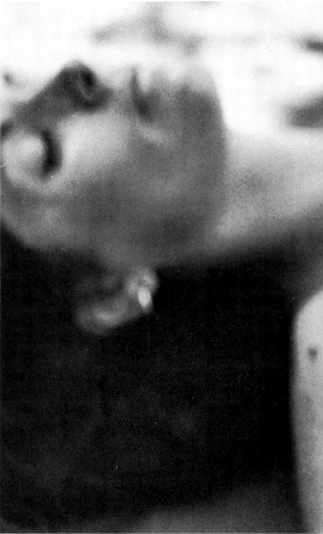

tenderness bathing

----

while the receiving
partner undresses
and gets settled
the giving partner
gets a bowl
of warm water
and a wash cloth
when both are ready
the active partner

slowly tenderly bathes
every inch
of his partner's body
don't talk
frequently rinse warm
your wash cloth
after doing both sides
and giving your partner
a chance to experience
digest the effects
change places

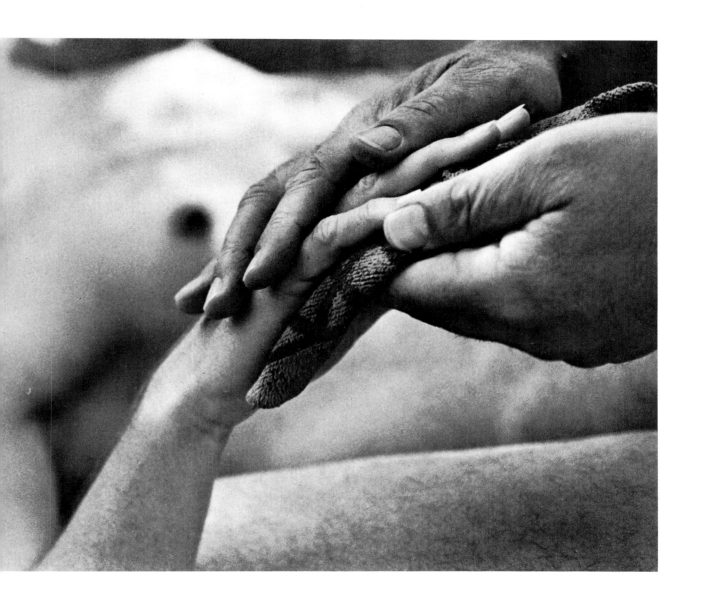

close embrace being

both partners stand up
one partner closes
his eyes and is
slapped from
head to toe
by the other
after allowing the
receiving partner
time to absorb
the experience
exchange roles and
the other partner
is slapped
then without talking
and moving as little
as possible
lie in each others arms
face to face
for 5 to 10 minutes
and feel what's
happening
the energy warmth
between you

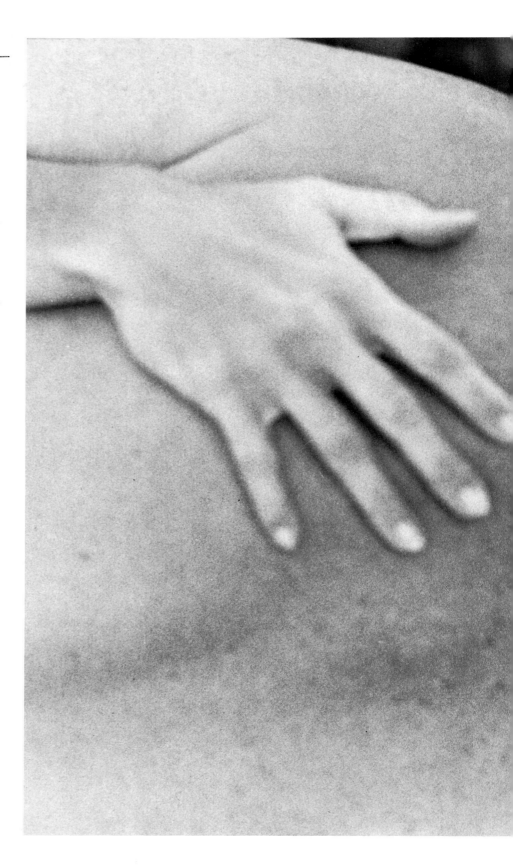

it's
hot fudge
sunday
lying
next to you
i'm so
warm flow

happy

feed your partner

one partner
is fed a meal
by the other partner
there is no talking
during this experience
at times the person
being fed
closes his eyes
after
switch roles
don't discuss your
experience until
both have finished
feeding each other

read
study
absorb

watts:
nature
man and
woman

deutsch:
the key to
feminine response
in marriage

M.D.scover
_____

sex
is not
dirty
or nasty
but an art
which requires
training
understanding
knowledge
feeling skill

play doctor
patient with
your mate
examine see
feel explore
talk about
the various parts
functions
of each others body

candle light hearted
_____

share an evening
together
with just candles
and other
natural sources
of light
alone with
one another
without any
outside distractions

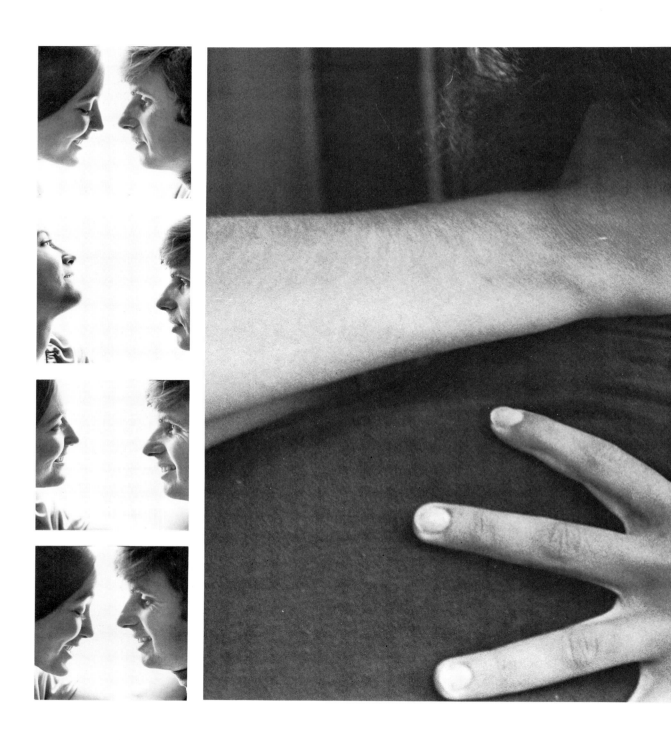

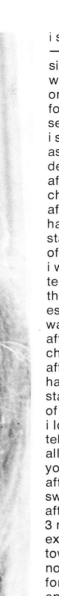

i see i want i love

---

sit knee to knee
with your partner
on the floor
for 3 minutes repeat
sentences starting with
i see
as you do so
describe your partner
after 3 minutes
change roles
after the second partner
has had a turn
start a new series
of sentences with
i want
tell your partner
the things you
especially
want from him
after 3 minutes
change roles
after the second partner
has had a turn
start another series
of sentences with
i love
tell your partner
all the things
you love about him
after 3 minutes
switch roles
after the second
3 minutes
express how you feel
toward your partner
non verbally
for 3 minutes
and then you may
discuss the experience
if you want to

physical love
can be taught
learned in a positive
rather than
negative manner

you don't do it
with every/body
not because it's
dirty or bad

but because
it's something
special

a mind/body/spiritual
closeness contemplation

an exchange of vibration

energy sharing
worship
intimacy

deep feeling

communication

understanding
caring
meditation

practice
patience
love

an extension
of self/fullness

mutual wisdom

realizations
in relations

the pubococcygeus
(p.c.)
surrounds
and lies inside of
the sphincter muscles
which close the outer
openings of the urinary
passage rectum and
birth canal
the fibers of this thick
muscle runs
from the pubis
the bony prominence at
the front of the pelvis
to the coccyx
the end of the spine

learning to contract
tone this muscle
according to kagel:
not only improves
the support given
the organs of the pelvis
but can enhance
sexual pleasure
responsiveness in
intercourse
and help promote
orgasm in women
in men strengthening
the p.c. can help to
extend the period
before ejaculation

awareness of this
muscle
and the type
of contractions
necessary
for exercising and
strengthening it
can best be experienced
by interrupting the flow
of urination
while sitting on
the toilet
with your knees
spread apart

the p.c. is not
the external muscles
of the vaginal opening
or the muscles which
lift and contract
the anus
but the intrinsic muscles
of the pelvis floor
the correct exercise
motion for strengthening
and toning this muscle
is a tightening

contraction
which moves the
inner pelvic wall forward
when released
it returns to its
normal position

each contraction
is held for 2 seconds

start with 5 to 10
contractions

do 10 before
getting out of bed
in the morning
and the same number
at 6 different intervals
during the day
do another 10
in bed before going
to sleep

it is desirable
to practice this
exercise whenever
you urinate

build from 10 to 20
and then 30
contractions at a time

though at first the
exercise
will require
concentration
it will soon become
almost effortless

they can be done
without being noticed
any where

it is rewarding
to contract the p.c.
before and during
intercourse

you will note
sexual
and other changes
in 3 weeks time
but continue to practice
200 to 300 contractions
a day

after 6 to 10 weeks
further exercise is
usually
not necessary for
once strengthened
the p.c. tends to
maintain
its own tone
aided by involuntary
contractions
during sexual climax

both partners
especially women
ask/tell your partner
precisely
what you want
what stimulates you

don't expect
your mate to magically
or intuitively
know your
desires/needs

telling one another
verbally as well as
non/verbally
will enhance
your intimacy dance

realize
you can kiss
touch play
without going
all the way
physical love is not
a compulsive need
to prove anything
but an intimate
artful way
to communicate
convey

come union

love is care
care for one another

care
FULLY

massage

**it is better
to give
and receive**

MASSAGE is
a universal language
a dancing series
of brush strokes
designed
to regenerate
the entire mind/body

an active meditation

to increase
circulation
muscular rehabilitation
relaxation
energy stimulation
mind/body integration
awareness

delight

sensation

what's important is
feeling sensitivity
not technique

communication

contact wisdom
without words

glowing
lowing

experience
care

and being

cared
for

INSTRUCTIONS FOR
THE PERSON GIVING
A MASSAGE

do the movements
with a flowing
consistent speed

pressure is a matter
of individual strength
and preference

if you are not sure about
the amount of pressure
to use ask your partner

TALK AS LITTLE
AS POSSIBLE

do each sequence
at least 3 times
unless otherwise
instructed

always increase
pressure
each time you repeat
a sequence
first time: light
second time: medium
third time: heavy
unless otherwise
directed

MASSAGE TOWARD
THE HEART
whenever possible

at times work
with your eyes closed

every inch of the body
will respond to your
hands
working in one place
will often bring about
a release in another
do each area well
without spending
too much or too little
time with any one
though oil is
all you really need
it is desirable
to have
soap and water
or rubbing alcohol
sheets and towels

the best place
to give a massage is
in a warm quiet room
or out doors
in the sun

spread a clean sheet
over a massage table
a bed the floor or grass

you may want to cover
your partner with
another sheet

keep some towels handy

wash your hands
with soap and water
or rubbing alcohol

warm/energize your
hands
by rubbing them
together and/or
do finger
energy flicks

use coconut oil or
vegetable oil or
a mixture of
2/3 vegetable oil
1/3 baby oil
and a few drops of
oil of clove

warming the oil
is an added treat

pour the oil
on to your hands and
gently vigorously caress
the area of your
partner's body
using circular
and stroking motions

use only enough oil
to give the skin
a glossy shine
so that your hands
slide freely

to cut down friction
more oil is needed
in areas
that are extra hairy

it is not necessary
or always desirable
to massage
the entire body
and often
concentrating
on one area or
a number of small ones
will provide great
relaxation and
satisfaction
this is especially true
of the neck shoulders
hands feet and back

don't rush

be sublime

give

TAKE YOUR
ETERNAL TIME

instructions for the
person receiving a
massage

if possible
take a warm bath
and soak for
5 to 10 minutes
before your treatment

it is preferable
that you disrobe
completely
for your massage
if this is uncomfortable
respect your resistance
either talk/work through
this feeling
with your partner
or wear a bathing suit

if there is a
special area of tension
a place or places
you would like
to have emphasized
let your partner know

if your partner
is working with
too much
or too little pressure
in any given area or
in general
be sure to verbally
or non/verbally
let him know

keep your eyes closed
as much as possible

talk as little
as necessary

you don't have to help
do anything
while being massaged
just be aware

breathe
easy
flow

just
let yourself

glow

the 3 basic strokes
used with
slight variation
all over the body are:

stroking
thumbs out
wringing

the 3 basic strokes
used on the neck are:

circles
down over around
and up
3 lifts

the 3 basic strokes
used over the hands
are:

corkscrew
thumbs up
palm twist

the 3 basic strokes
used on the feet are:

corkscrew
thumbs up
heel palm twist

the partner
to be massaged
lies down
on his back
allow him at least
1 minute
to get with himself
while you prepare
yourself
and oil your hands
then oil the back
and side
of your partner's
neck and shoulders

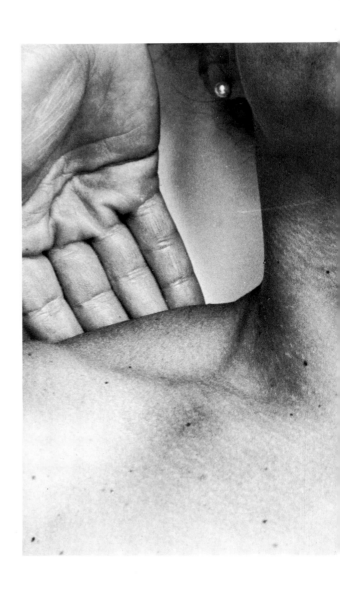

circles (back shoulder
neck)

place your finger tips
on the beginning points
of the trapizius
(outer bottom tip
of the shoulders) and
in a continuous motion
make small
moderately fast
circles over the back
of this muscle
toward the neck
continue the circles
up the back of the neck
just before
you reach the hair line
take your fingers away
from the neck and
make a half circle
through the air
to your partner's
shoulders
so that your hands
come back to the
starting point on the
acromion process

repeat the sequence
of circles
over the shoulders
and neck

this movement is done
½ dozen times
lightly the first
2 times
medium the second
2 times
heavier the last
2 times

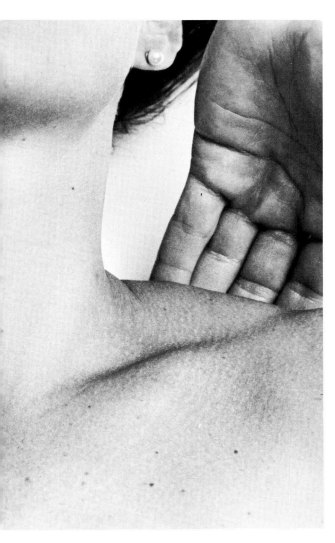

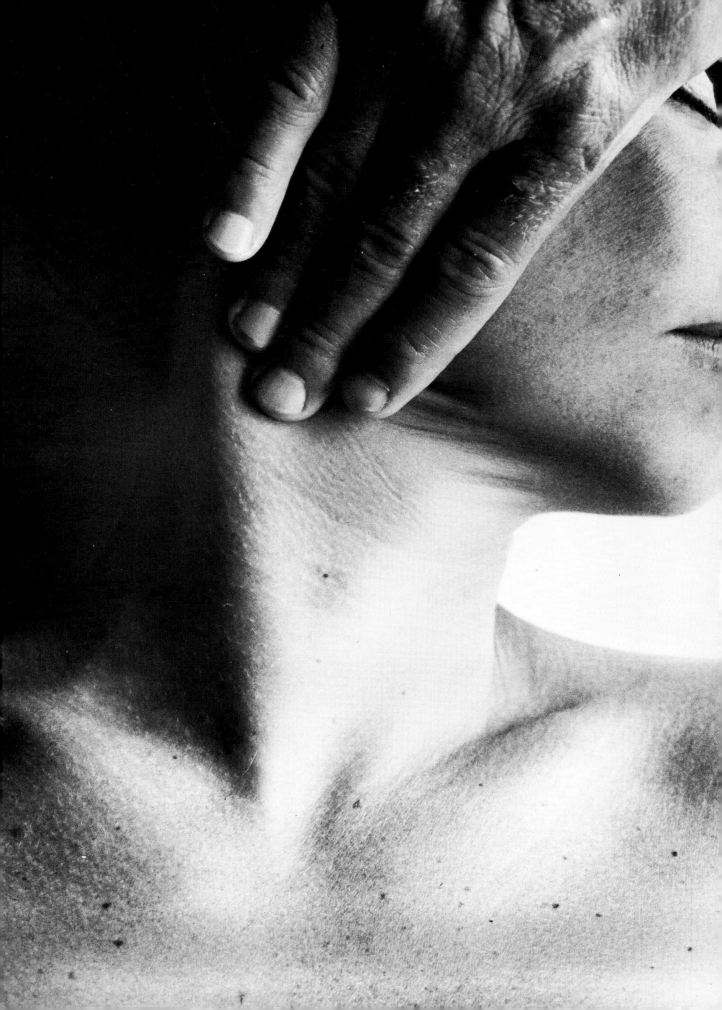

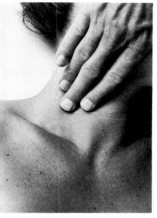
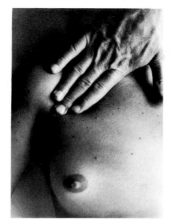
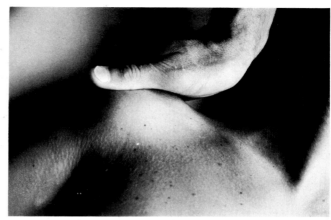

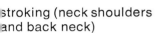

stroking (neck shoulders
and back neck)

with a feeling of
assurance
take hold and lift
your partner's head
with both your hands
lift it up 2 inches
turn his head to the left
your left hand supports
his head and
comes to rest
on the table
with your right hand
you stroke gently
firmly from just under
your partner's ear
(mastoid process)
down over the side
of the neck
lessen pressure when
you reach upper chest
so you can go
over the clavical bone
on the upper chest
around the shoulder
then with a firmer
pressure move
over the back trapizius
and up the back of
your partner's neck
when you reach
the hairline
take your hands away
and again place them
in the starting position

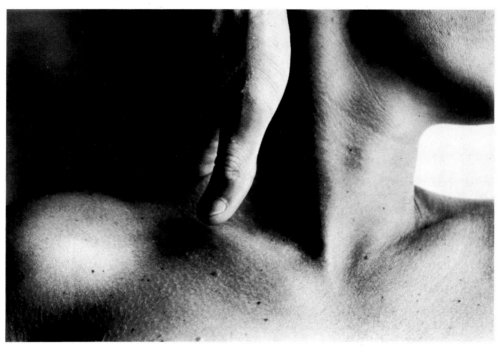

repeat the stroke
2 more times

after take hold
of your partner's head
with both your hands
again
and turn it
to the right
your right hand supports
the head
while your left hand
repeats the stroke

oil the left hand
and fingers

corkscrew (fingers)

_____

place your
index finger under
and your thumb above
the tip of your
partner's little finger
your index finger
is used largely
to support and keep
the finger straight
firmly use a continuous
twisting corkscrew
motion
up the finger
when you reach
the hand
in a continuous motion
milk down the bottom
top of the finger
to the starting point
your other hand
supports
your partner's wrist

repeat this motion
up and down
each finger
3 times

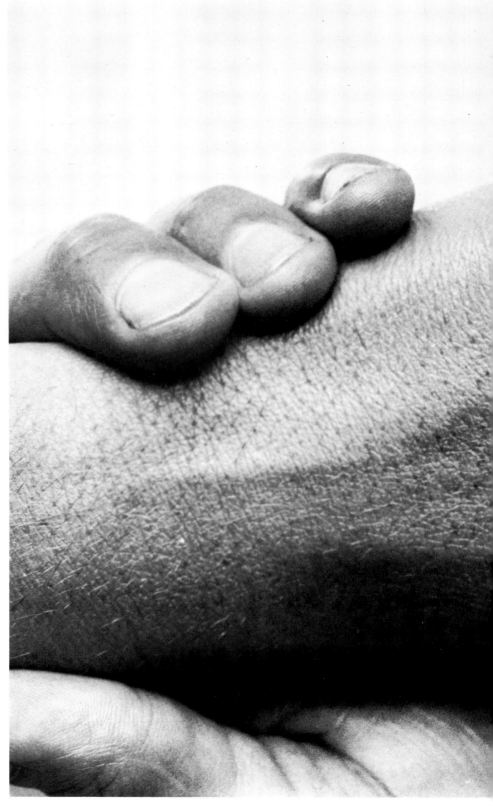

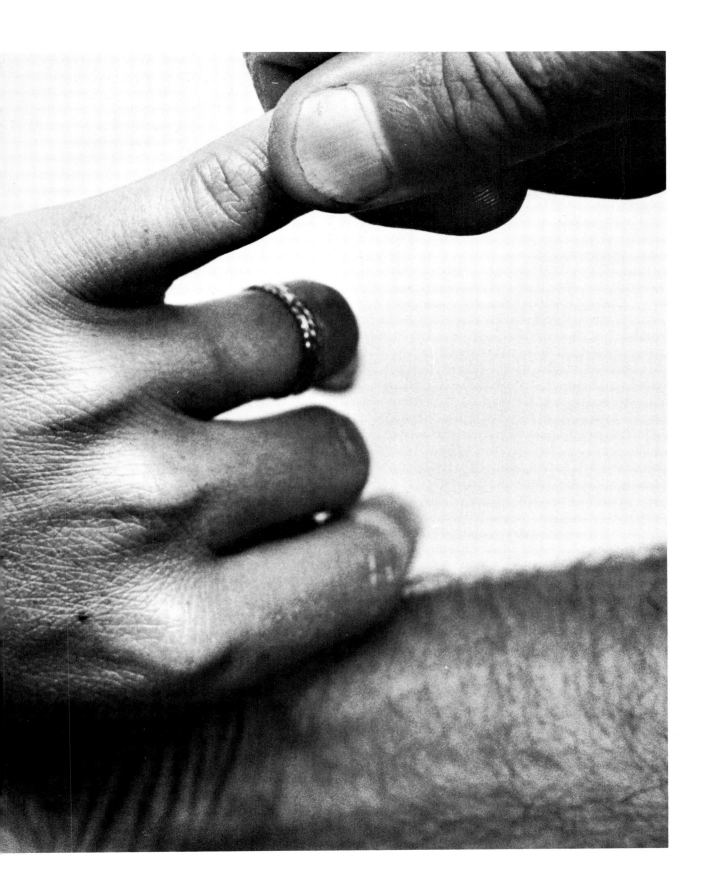

 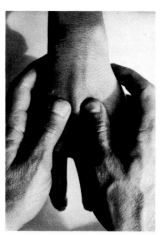 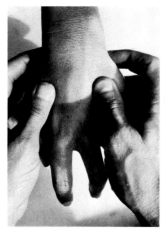 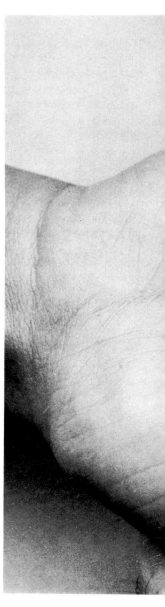

thumbs up (palm and
back of hand)

take hold
of your partner's hand
and sensitively turn
the hand over
palms down
place both your thumbs
together at the center
of the base
of the hand
your fingers go
around the sides and
under the hand
with pressure on your
thumb tips
stroke straight up
the hand to the wrist
now with slightly

less pressure
bring the thumbs
straight back down
to the base of the hand
when you come back
to the starting point
move both your thumbs
½ inch toward the
outside
of the hand and
repeat the stroke up
and down the hand
when you again
come back
down to the base
move your thumbs
another ½ inch toward
the outside of the hand
and repeat
the up and down stroke

then when you reach
the base
move your thumbs
to the center of the hand
where you started

repeat the above
sequence
over the hand
2 more times

increase pressure
in each new sequence

turn the hand over
palms up and
repeat the same
procedure

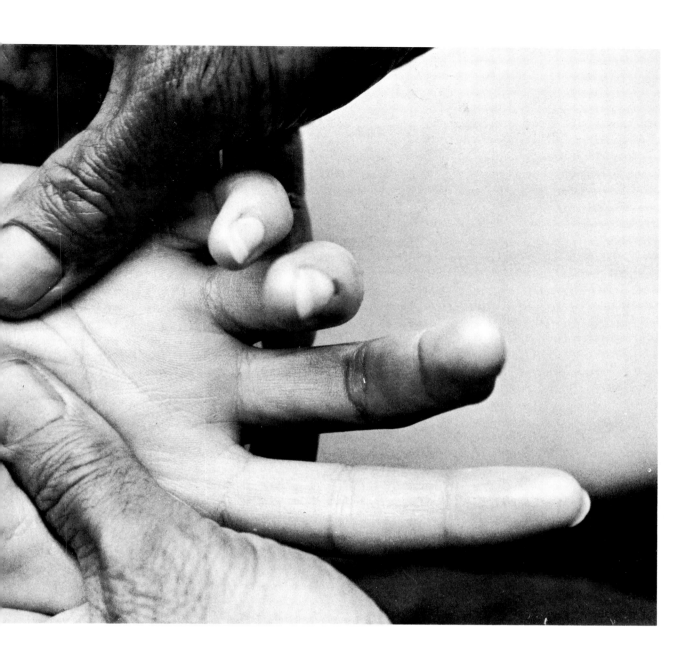

hand (heel/palm twist)

place your thumbs
over your partner's
thumb base
press the heel
of your hand
over your partner's heel
(mound of Venus)
your palm and fingers
are just over the edge
(your other hand
supports
your partner's hand)
slide your palm over
your partner's
palm/heel
using the base of
his thumb
as a pivot point
using a strong
continuous pressure
slide your
heel/palm
back and forth
6-9 times over
your partner's
palm/heel
the movement/pressure
will create a kind of
vacuum suction
make sure the pressure
and motion
are continuous

oil left arm
wrist to shoulder

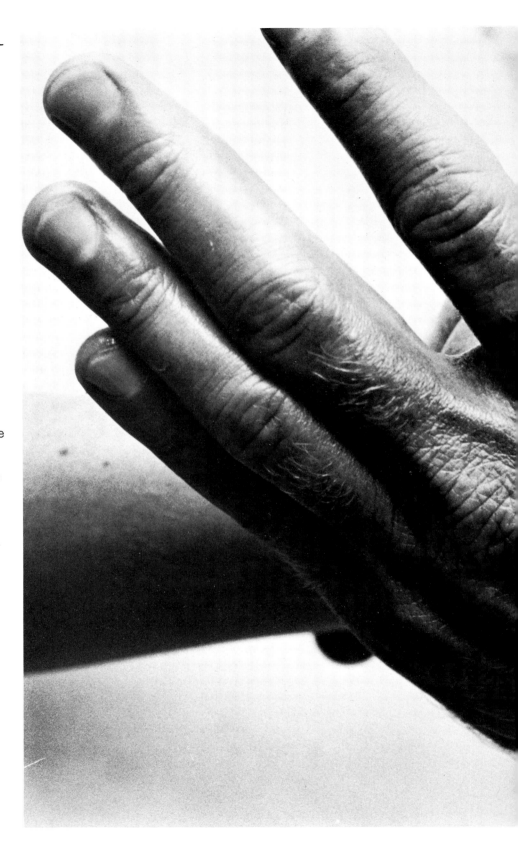

stroking (arms)

place your left hand
palm down
on your partner's
left wrist
let your hand
take the shape of
the area
you are touching
the right hand goes
in front of
your left hand
fingers face in
opposite directions
with a firm
steady pressure
slide both hands
up the arm
when you reach
the shoulder
separate the hands
the hand closest
to the body
goes across the arm pit
and down the inside
of the arm
simultaneously
the other hand goes
around the shoulder and
down the outside
of the arm
when both hands
reach the wrist
the stroke is repeated

repeat each stroke
a minimum of 3 times

use a little more
pressure
each time you go
up the arm

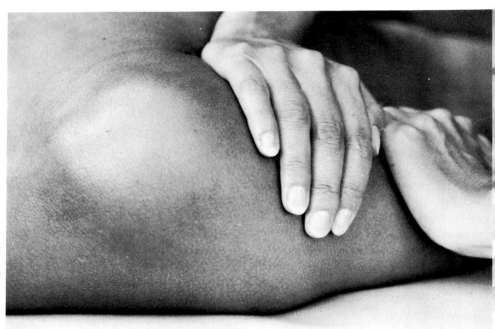

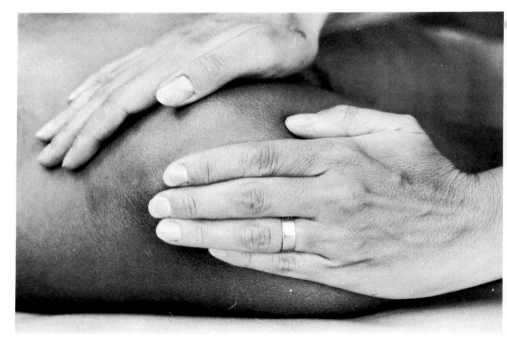

thumbs out (arms)

place your thumbs
on top of
your partner's wrist
(which is palm down)
your palms surround
the sides of the wrist
fingers underneath
move your hands and
fingers
up the arm
as the thumbs separate
and move out across
the top and side
of the wrist
forearm and upperarm
after each downward
stroke
with your thumbs
slide your hands
up the arm ¼ inch
repeat the stroke
up the arm with
your thumbs
when you reach the
shoulder
slide down the inside
and outside of the arm
as you did in stroking

keep the pressure
constant
within a sequence

repeat these
thumb separations
all the way up the arm
at least 3 times

use a little more
pressure
each time you go
up the arm

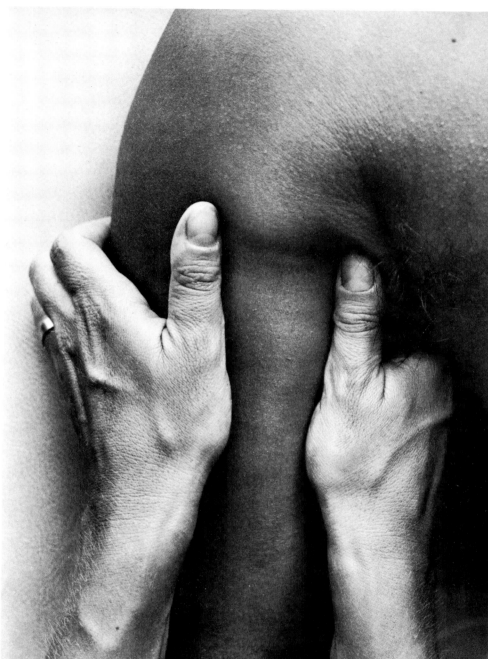

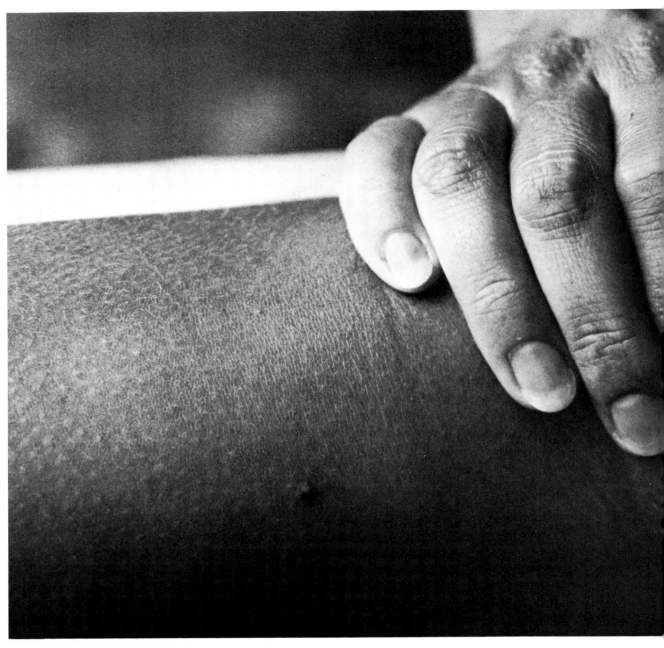

wringing (arms)

face the side
of your partner's arm
and place your hands
side by side
over his left wrist
thumbs on top next to
the other fingers
now simultaneously
slide your
right hand away from
left hand toward

your body and
bring them back to
center
then simultaneously
slide your
left hand away from
right hand toward
your body and
bring them back to
center
this motion is continued
all the way up the arm
now with slightly

less pressure
slide down
the arm to the wrist

repeat this movement
a minimum of 3 times

increase pressure
each time

oil and massage
right hand and arm
in the same order

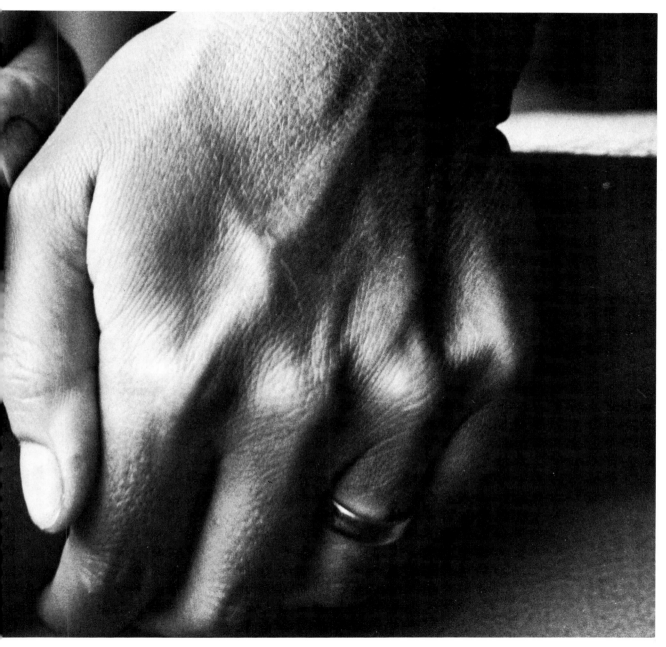

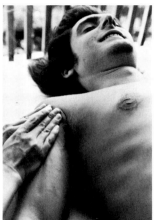

oil the left foot

corkscrewing (toes)

_____

place your
index finger under
and your thumb above
the little toe
your index finger is
used largely
to support and
keep the toe straight
(because of the size
it is difficult to
corkscrew a toe
do the best you can)
with your other hand
hold the foot steady
firmly use a continuous
twisting corkscrew
motion
up the toe
when you reach
the foot
in a continuous motion
milk down the toe
to the starting position
don't twist the toe

repeat this motion
up and down
each toe
3 times

thumbs up (top and
bottom of feet)

_____

place your thumbs
tips together
on the center base of
your partner's foot
your fingers are around
the bottom of the foot
with pressure slide
your thumbs up
to the ankle
when you reach the top
with slightly less
pressure
bring the thumbs
straight down
to the base
of the foot
when you are back
at the starting position
move both thumbs
½ inch
toward the outside
of the foot
and repeat the
up and down stroke
once more
when you again
come back down
move the thumbs
another ½ inch toward
the outside of the foot
and repeat
the up and down stroke
once more
then when you reach
the base
slide your thumbs
back to the center
thumbs touching
the way you started

repeat the above
sequence
over the foot
2 more times

increase pressure
in each new sequence

turn around and repeat
the above sequence
on the bottom
of the foot
starting from the
base below the toes
to the heel of the foot

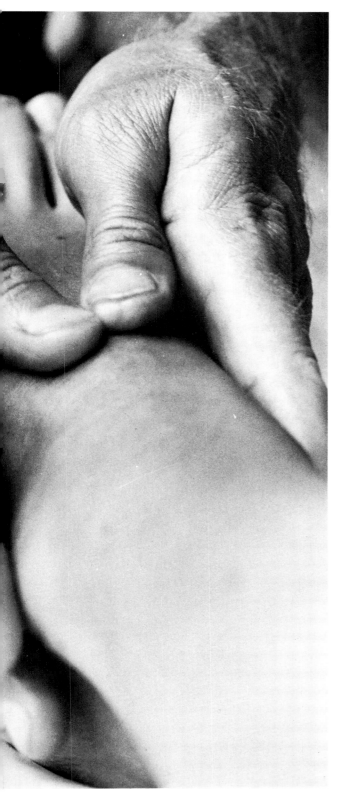

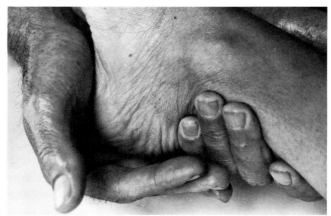

palm twist (heel of foot)

lift and hold your
partner's left leg
with your left hand
place the palm of
your right hand on
your partner's heel
and with a strong
steady pressure
twist turn your hand
(don't twist the heel)
repeat the twist
6 to 9 times
in a continuous motion
then put the leg down

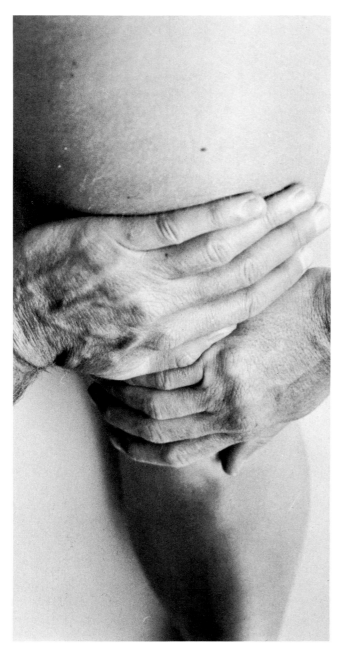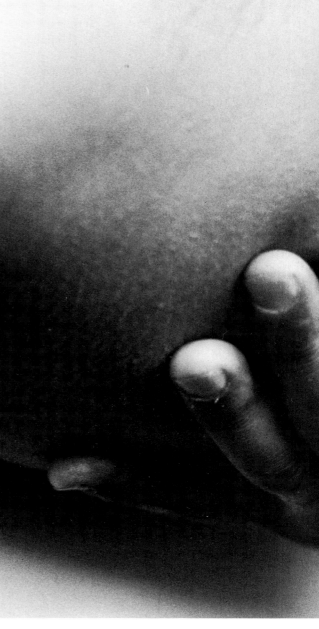

the front of the legs
ankle to hip
are oiled and massaged
with the same
3 basic strokes
as the arm
the only differences are
that because
the shin bone
covers the
lower leg muscles
from the ankle
to the knee
the thumbs out

and wringing motion
are done
from the knee up only
the stroking movement
however
is over the full length
of the leg

because of the size
of the leg
it will require
more pressure
than you used
on the arms

stroking (front leg)
————————————————

place your left hand
palm down
on your partner's
left ankle
let your hand
take the shape
of the area you are
touching
the right hand goes
in front of the left
the fingers face
in opposite directions

with a firm steady
pressure
slide both hands up
the leg
when you reach the
upper limit of the thigh
separate the hands
the hand closest to
the midline comes down
the inside of the thigh
simultaneously
the other hand goes
down the outside
of the thigh

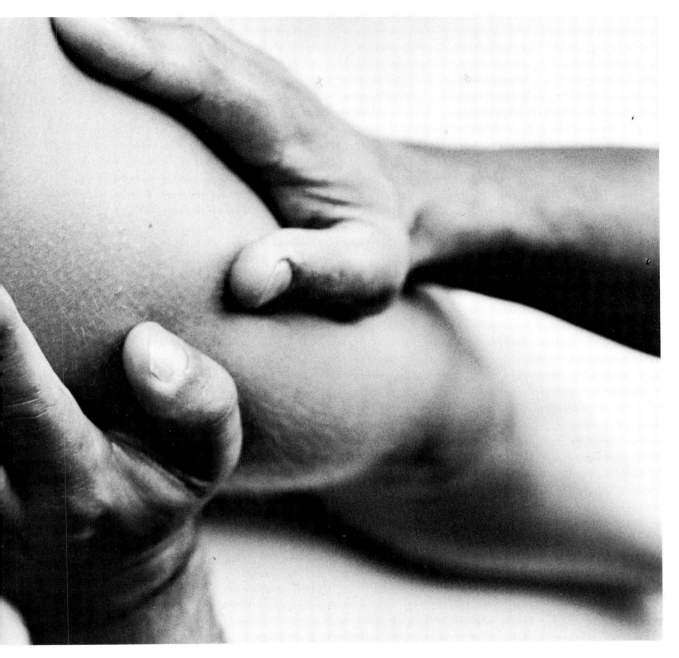

when both hands reach
the ankle
the stroke is repeated

repeat each stroke
a minimum of 3 times

use more pressure
each time you go
up the leg

use a firm though
lighter pressure
going down the leg

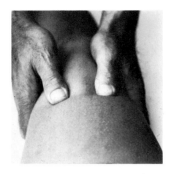

thumbs out (front leg)

place your thumbs
together
on top of your
partner's thigh
just above the knee
your hands are around
the sides
fingers underneath
move your hands
and fingers
up the thigh
as the thumbs separate
and move out across
the top and sides
of the thigh
after each
downward stroke
with your thumbs
slide your hands up
the thigh ½ inch and
repeat the stroke
up the leg with
your thumbs
when you reach the top
of the thigh
slide down
the inside and outside
of the thigh
as you did
in stroking

repeat the entire
sequence
of these thumb
separations
all the way up the thigh
at least 3 times

use a little more
pressure
each time you
go up the thigh

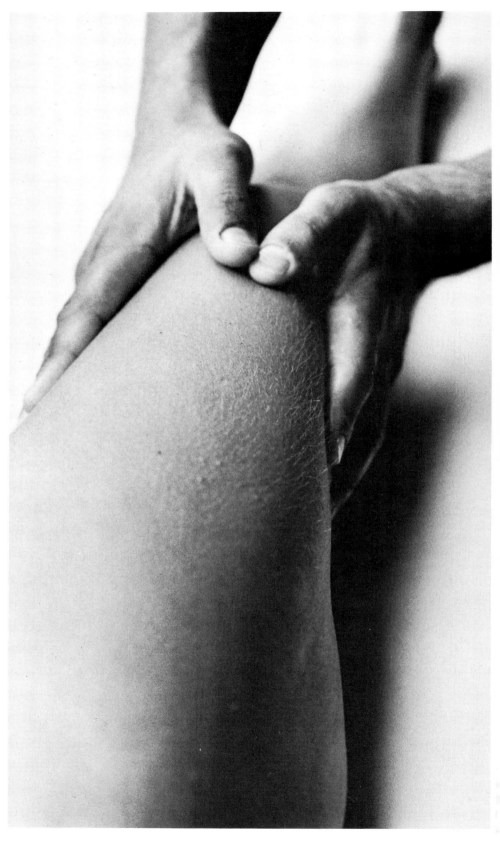

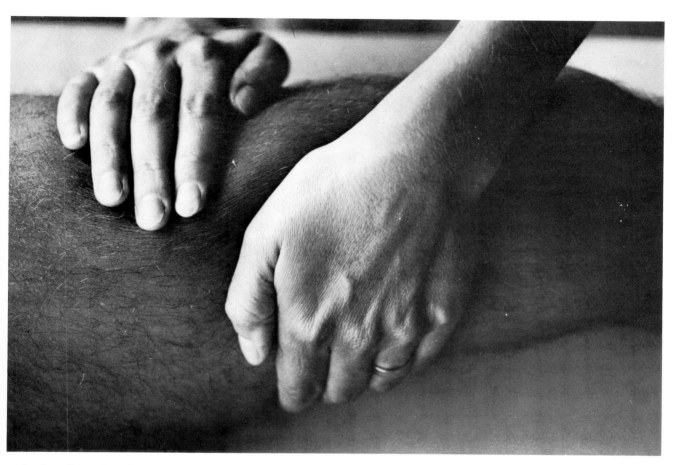

wringing (front legs)

face the side of
your partner's leg and
place both hands
side by side
over the thigh
just above the knee
thumbs on top next to
the other fingers
now simultaneously
slide your
right hand away from
left hand toward
your body and
bring them
back to center
then simultaneously
slide your
left hand away from
right hand toward
your body and
bring them
back to center
this motion is continued
all the way up the leg

now with slightly
less pressure
when you reach the top
of the thigh
slide down
the inside and outside
of the thigh

repeat this sequence
a minimum of 3 times

increase pressure
each time

oil and massage
right foot and leg
in the same order

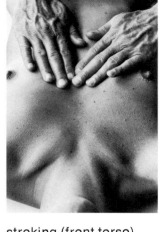

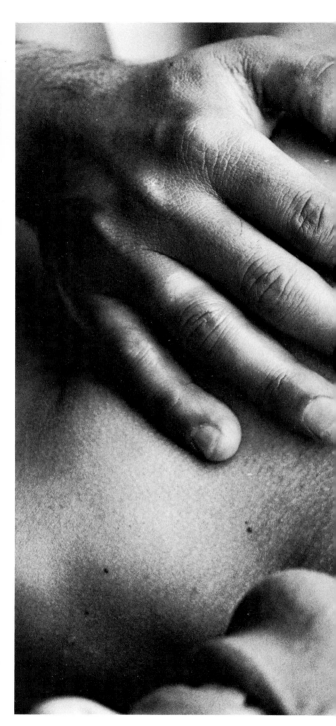

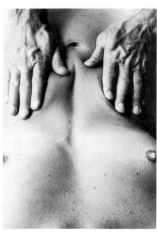

oil and massage
the torso
with essentially the
same 3 strokes
the major difference is
that because the torso
is larger than
the arms or legs
stroking is modified
thumbs out becomes
palms out
and wringing becomes
crossing

stroking (front torso)
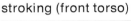

place your hands flat
on top of the
lower abdomen
with the tips
of the thumbs
touching each other
and with a
firm steady pressure
slide your hands up
the stomach and
bring your hands
together and go
over the chest
of your partner
as you reach the
shoulders
separate your hands
continue the motion
around
the upperchest
and bring
both hands down
the side
of your partner's torso
when you reach
the lower abdomen
bring your hands
back to the
starting position
begin the next stroke
up the torso

repeat the stroke
2 more times

use a little more
sensitivity
pressure each time
you go
up and down the torso

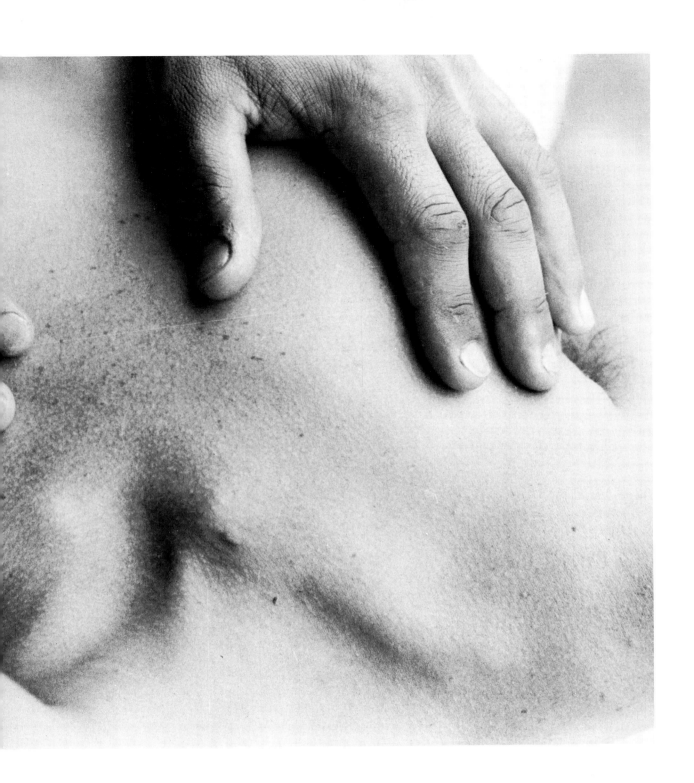

palms out (front torso)

place the heel of
your hands on the
center of your
partner's abdomen
the hands are flat
fingers point out to
the sides
slide the heel and palm
of your hand over to
and down the side of
your partner's torso
take your hands
away from
the body and
bring the heel of
your hands back to the
center of the abdomen
½ inch above the
previous starting point
and make another
stroke

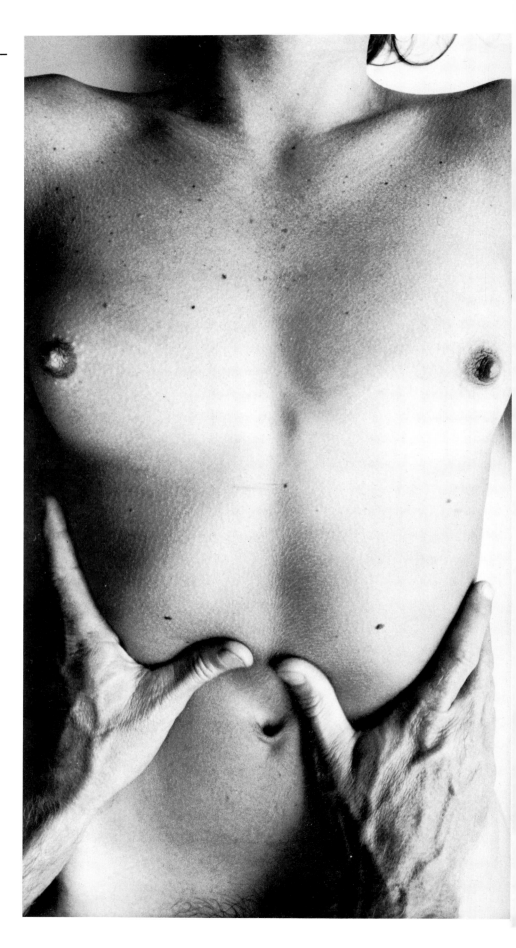

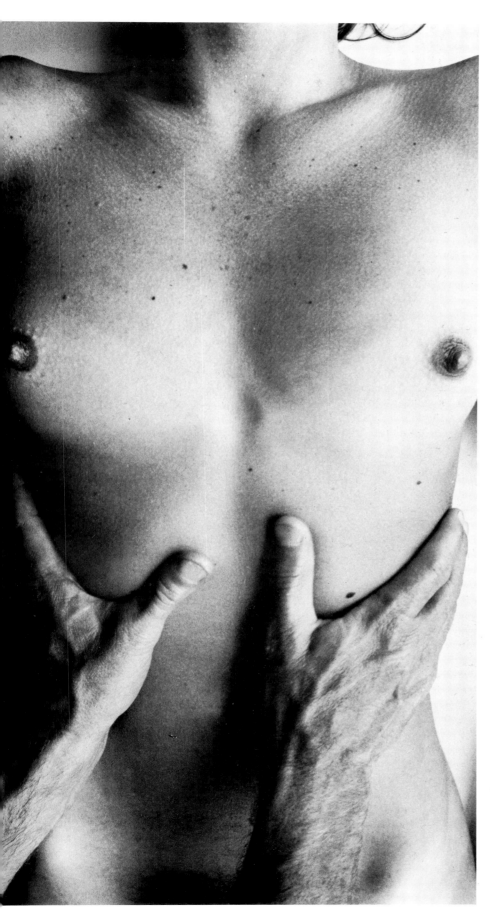

continue this movement
up the torso
and over
the chest
in the case of massaging
women with
large breasts
be especially
sensitive careful
when you reach the top
of the chest
rather than returning
to the center
your hands come down
the side of the torso
to the lower abdomen

repeat the stroke
2 more times

use a little more
pressure
each time you do an
entire sequence

crossing (front torso)

place hands thumbs
and fingers together
on the top
of your partner's
lower abdomen
now simultaneously
slide your right hand
away from
left hand toward
your body and
bring them back to
the center
then simultaneously
slide your left hand
away from your
right hand toward
your body and
bring them back to
the center
continue this sliding
movement up the torso
as in wringing
when you reach the top
of the chest
reverse the process
back down the torso
to the starting position
the pressure
going down
is the same as
going up
when massaging
a woman
be extra careful
and sensitive
or avoid the breasts

repeat the stroke
up and down the torso
3 times

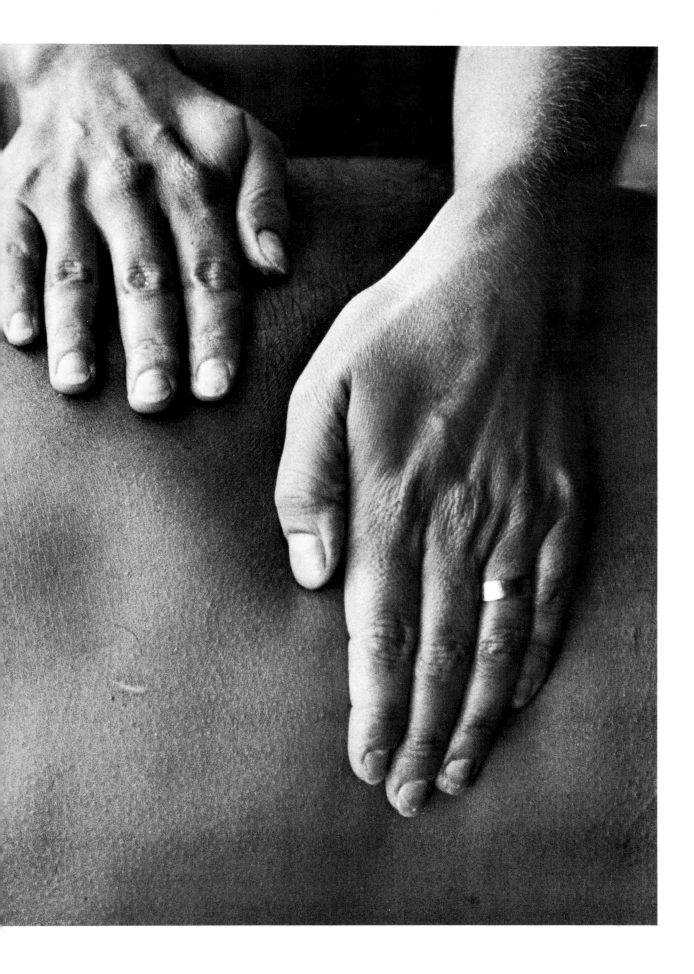

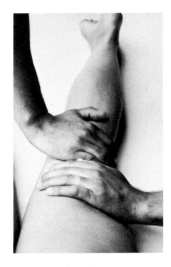 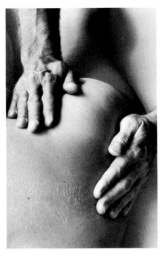 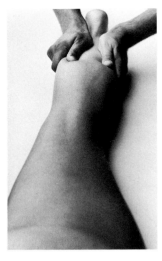

your partner turns over
on the front of
his body

oil back of
left leg and buttocks

stroking (back leg)

place your left hand
palm down on your
partner's left ankle
let your hand take
the shape of the area
you are touching
the right hand goes
in front of the left
fingers face in
opposite directions
with a firm
steady pressure
slide both hands
up the leg
and over the buttocks

in a half circle
the hand closest
to the midline comes
down
the inside of the leg
simultaneously
the outside hand goes
down
the outside of the leg
when you reach

the ankle
the stroke is repeated

repeat each stroke
a minimum of
3 times

each time you go
up the leg
increase the amount
of pressure you use

thumbs out (back leg)
_____

place your thumbs
together on top of
your partner's left ankle
your hands are around
the sides
fingers are under
the ankles
move the hands
and fingers
up the leg
as the thumbs
separate and move out
across the top and sides
of the leg
after each
downward stroke
with your thumbs
slide your hands up
the leg ½ inch
repeat the stroke with
your thumbs
when you reach

the bottom
slide down the
inside and the outside
of the leg
as you did in stroking

repeat the thumb
separations
up the leg
2 more times

use more pressure
in each of the
3 sequences
up the leg

use a good solid
pressure coming
down the leg

wringing (back leg)

face the side of
your partner's leg
and place both hands
side by side
over his left ankle
one hand ahead of
the other
thumbs on top next to
the other fingers
now simultaneously
slide your right
hand away from
left hand toward
your body and
bring them back to
center
then simultaneously
slide your left
hand away from
right hand toward

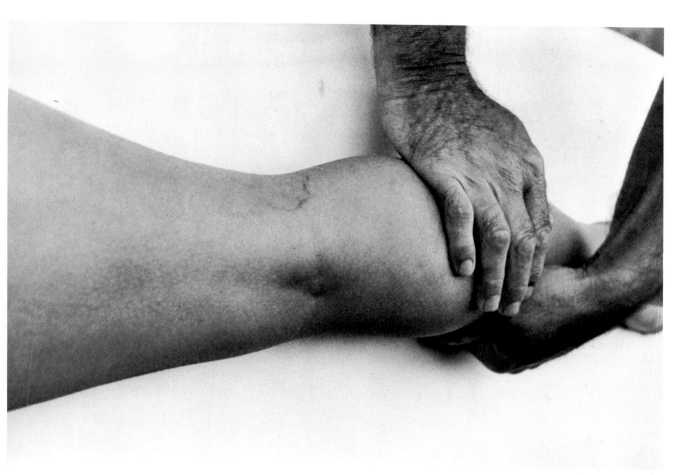

your body and
bring them back to
center
this movement is
continued up
the leg
when you reach the top
with slightly less
pressure slide back
down the leg

repeat this sequence a
minimum of 3 times

increase pressure
each time you go
up and down the
entire leg

oil and massage
right leg and buttock
in the same order

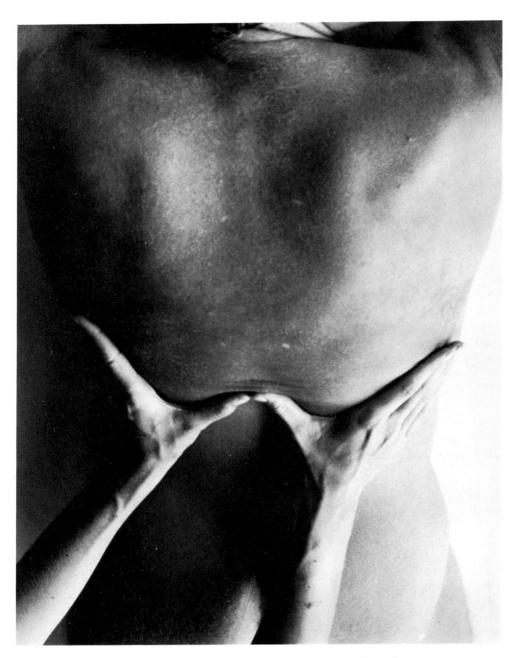

stroking (up the back)

---

place your hands flat
on your partner's
lower back in the
valley of the spine
with the finger tips
touch facing each other
use a firm
steady pressure
to slide your hands
up over your
partner's back
as you reach the
shoulders
your hands separate
in a continuous motion
around the shoulders
bring both hands down
the side of the back
when you reach the
lower back
your hands return to
the starting position

repeat this movement
2 more times

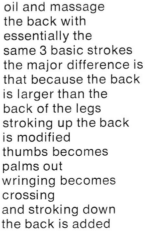

oil and massage
the back with
essentially the
same 3 basic strokes
the major difference is
that because the back
is larger than the
back of the legs
stroking up the back
is modified
thumbs becomes
palms out
wringing becomes
crossing
and stroking down
the back is added

use slightly less
pressure
coming down than going
up

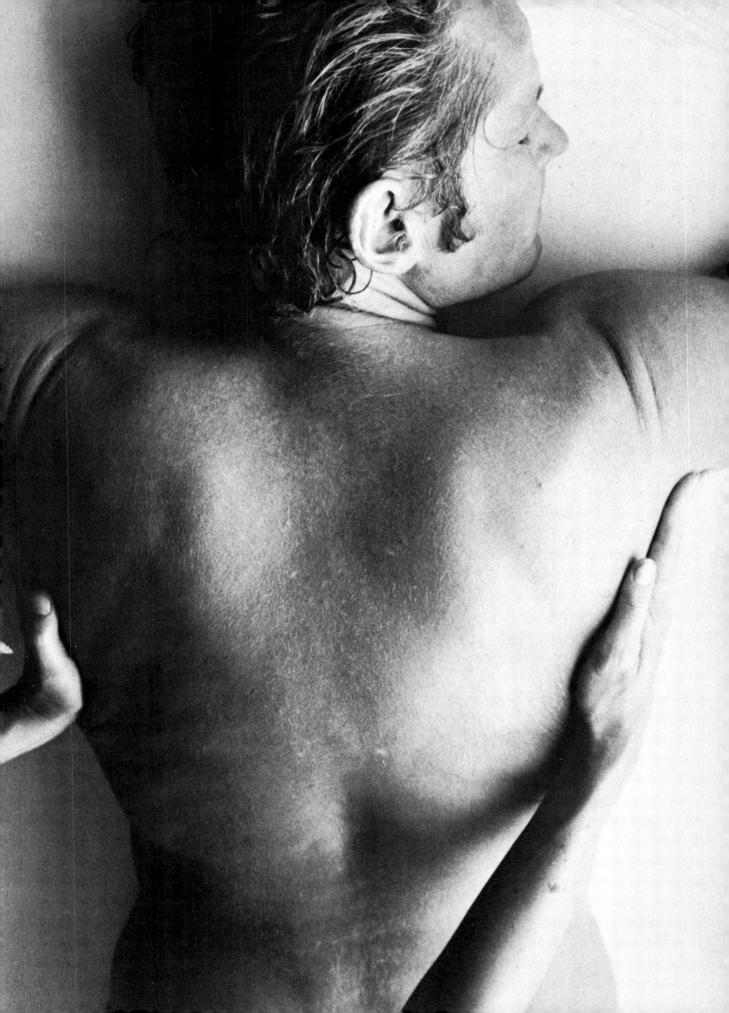

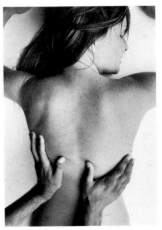
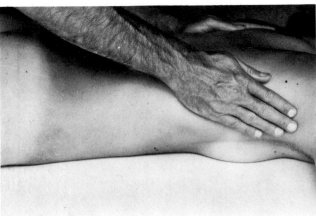
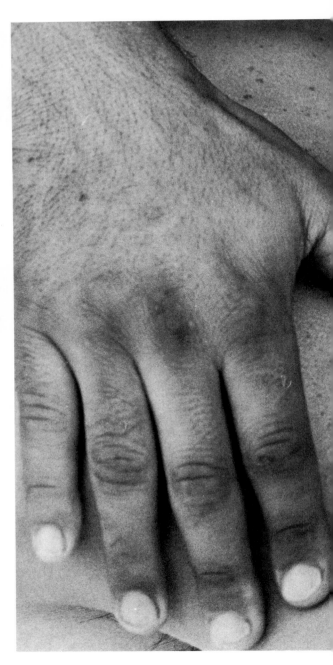

palms out (back)

place the palms and
fingers of your hands
on the center of your
partner's lower back
in the valley of the spine
the heels of the hands
touch one another
and your finger points
towards the side
of the body
slide the palms
of your hands
over the top and
down off the side of

your partner's body
return your hands to
the center of the back
½ inch above the
previous place and
you make
another stroke
continue this movement
up the back
with these ½ inch
spacings
when you reach the top
make a half circle
around the shoulders
and with both hands
come down the side of
your partner's back
when you reach the
lower back
bring your palms to
the starting position

repeat the entire
movement
up the back
2 more times
use a little more
pressure when coming
down the back

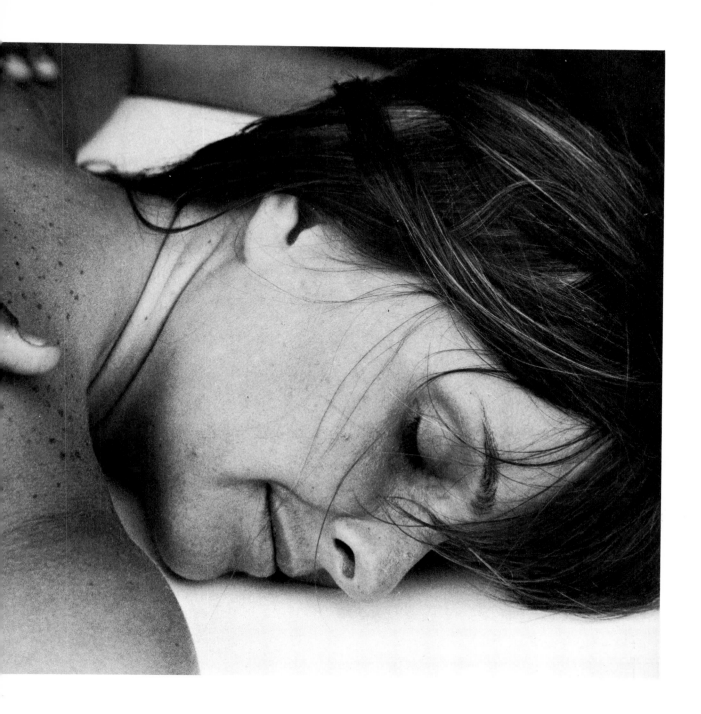

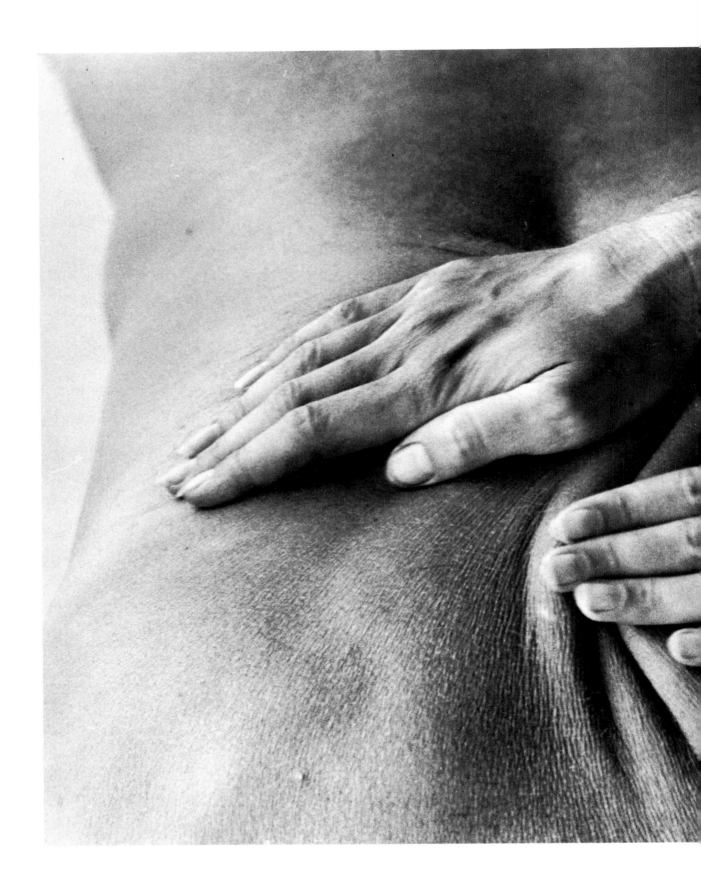

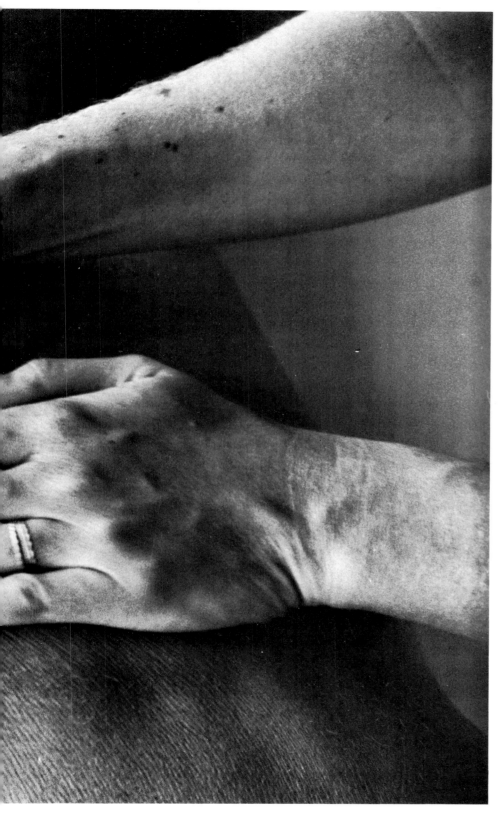

crossing (the back)

place hands fingers
and thumbs
together on top
in the center
of your partner's
lower back
now simultaneously
slide your
right hand away from
left hand toward
your body and
bring them back
to the center
then simultaneously
slide your
right hand toward
left hand away from
your body and
bring them back
to the center
continue this sliding
movement up the back
as in wringing
when you reach the top
of the back
reverse the process
down to the starting
position

the pressure
going down
is the same as going up
you move side to side
up and down the entire
back 3 times

stroking (down the back)

stand at the head
of the table
with the front of
your body facing
the top of your
partner's head
place both your hands
on his upper back
your hands are placed
so that the thumbs meet
in the center
the fingers are
slightly spread
slide both hands down
your partner's back
over around the

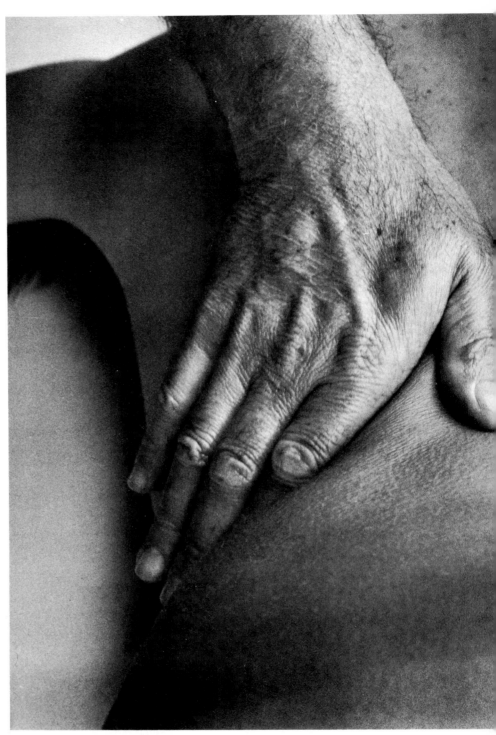

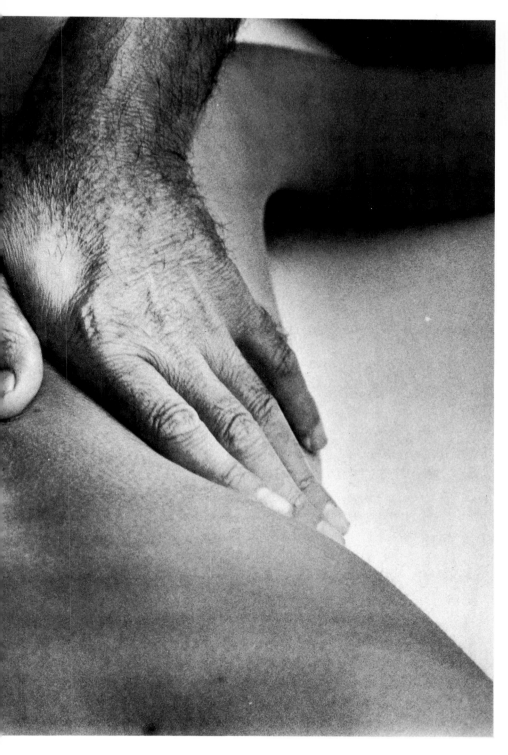

buttocks
your hands separate
and come up
the side
of your partner's
side back
when you reach the top
return to the
starting position

repeat the entire stroke
2 more times

the pressure on the
upward stroke is
almost as strong as
the pressure going
down

your partner turns over
on his back

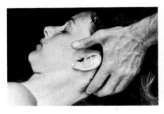

in the next two
movements
the receiving partner
allows his head to be
lifted turned and stroked
without hindering or
helping his partner

if the active partner
feels any help or
resistance while lifting
or turning
his partner's head
he pauses and waits
for a moment
before continuing
his movement

lifts (neck up and to the
side)
_____

with gentle authority
place both hands
on the back of the head
not the neck
cradle the head with
both hands
slowly lift the head
4 inches up
hold it there for
10 seconds
and then slowly lower it
back down to the table
and take
your hands away
give your partner time
to experience the lift
and then repeat it a
second time
the third time you lift
the head
half way up only
and supporting the head

slowly turn the head
gently
to the left as far as
it will go
without any pressure
the left hand support
the head
the right hand on the top
then slowly turn the
head
back to the center
after a moment pause
carefully
turn the head gently
to the right as far
as it will go
without pressure
the right hand supports
the head
the left hand is on top
hold it there for a
moment and
then turn it back to
center
be sure to keep the neck
in line
with the spine
repeat the left/right
turns in
each direction
lower the head back
down to
its resting place
and let your
partner have time to
digest the effects
lift lower and
turn the head
very slowly

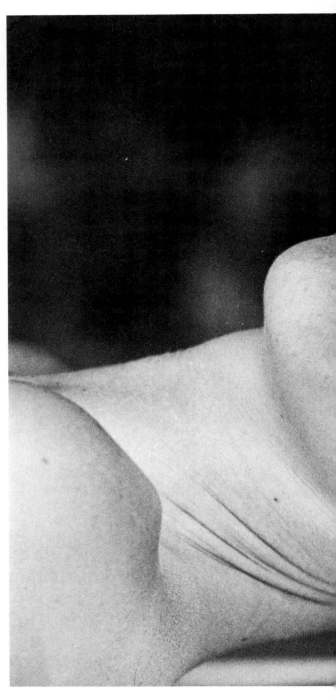

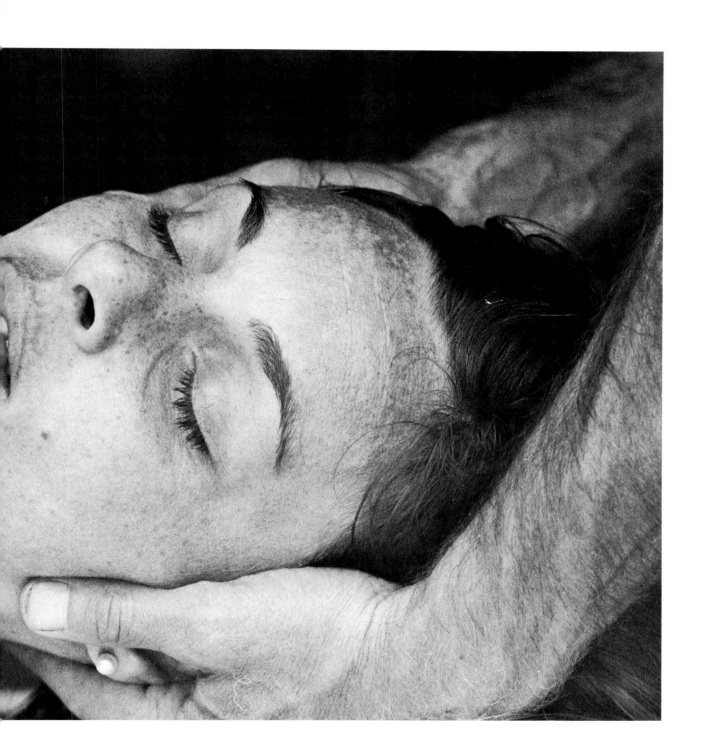

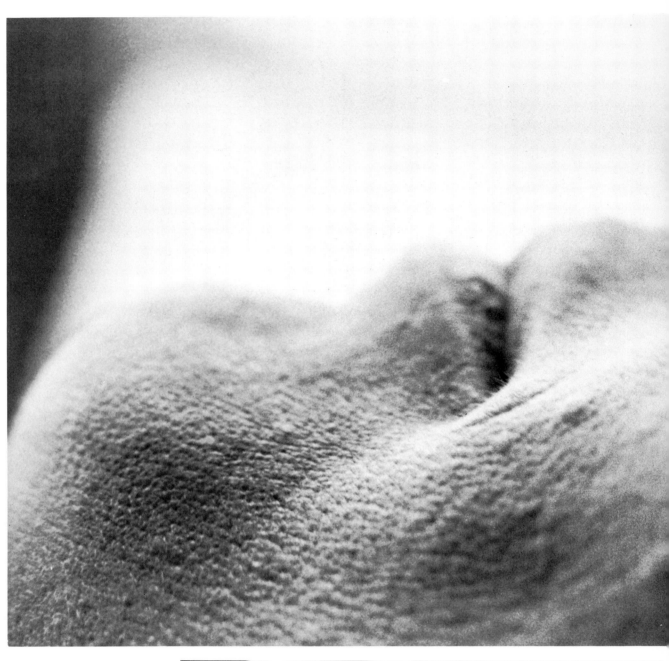
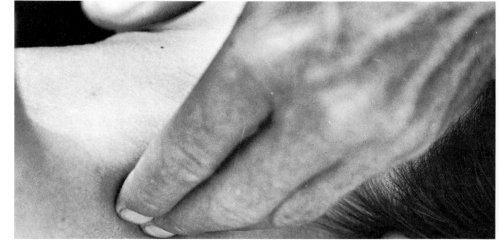

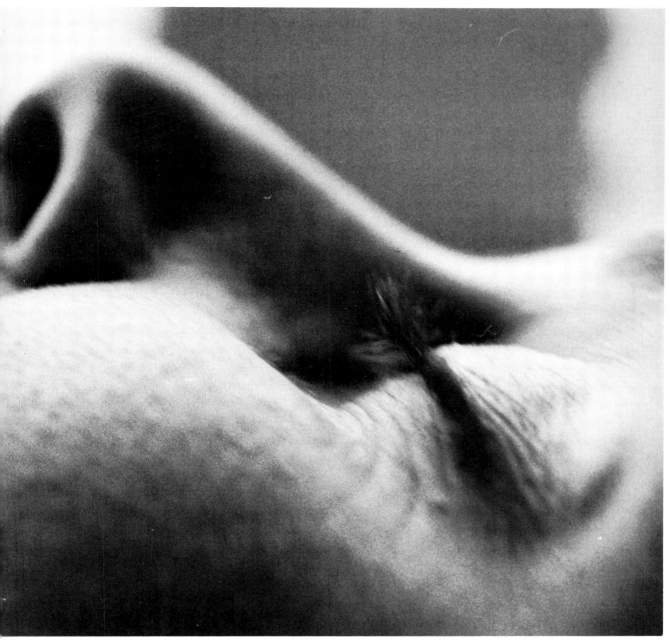

stroking (ironing back
of neck)

————————————————

place both hands under
the back of
your partner's
head and slowly lift it
half way up holding
the back of the head
securely with your
left hand
with your right hand
place the top 1/3 of your
fingers on the bottom
of the neck
stroke up the neck

shoulder to
back hair line
the motion from the
bottom to top is
continuous
with a firm
even pressure
each time
then place
your right hand
back on your partner's
head
this time
support the head
with your right hand
repeat the stroke 3 times

with your left hand
on the left side
of the neck
after place both hands
on the head
and lower it
to its resting place
move your hands away
and give your partner
a moment to integrate
the effects

REMEMBER
what's important
is SENSITIVITY

the procedure
given in this book
is a guide line
though it is desirable
that you learn and
in the beginning
do the movement
as indicated
once you have
mastered them
you can
substitute
eliminate
do any innovations
variations you
want to

just be aware

kept on its
highest level
massage is a peak
sensuous adventure
experience
the delight of light
texture color sound
smelling feeling
which can easily
lead to sexual arousal
especially if you
manipulate
your thoughts
your partner
in that direction

it's a question
of knowing

what your purpose is:

seduction

or

care
energy healing

relaxation
close feeling

all of the above

love

flo
we
R

return

i
die

and
am
set
free

and the energy
that was me

gradually

returns

to the source
of all bliss

no/thing/ness

death
is the
living
end

of this
physical
cycle

a reunion

to before
you were
born

from individuality

TOTALITY

I am
no longer

there are
two kinds
of death

symbolic
ego death

and the disintegration
of the physical body

ego death
is the giving up
of separate
consciousness

fusing with
the flow of the
universe/all

eventually
each wave
rejoins the sea
of energy

physical death
is the dis/appearance
of life

past/away
from this particular form

a transformation
an initiation
and eventual
reformation
in some other
manifestation

there is nothing
to fear

death is where
we came from

our fear of death
is conditioned
by our parents
culture thought
fright
and is related
to other fears
like being dropped
loss of support
past pain
injury suffering

physical death
is the end
of this round

a return to
before you
were born

a non/conflict
release

silence

eternal
peace

read

brown:
life against
death

elisabeth
kubler-ross:
on death
and dying

death experience
─────────────────
read
understand
memorize
the essence
of evans-wentzs
translation
of the
tibetan book
of the dead

make a pact
with some one
arrange to have them
read it to you
the appropriate parts
as a re/minder
while on the journey
of dying
just after you
are dead

will to be

as conscious

as you possibly can

realize that anything
everything you
experience
see is not reality
but the creation
of your own mind

scary as this may be
no harm can
come to you

move toward
the pure lights
as bright and blinding
as they may be

succeed and you
will be
eternally free

death

a time for
sorrow/joy
contemplation

good

mourning

grief

crying
is a relief

for those
remaining alive
a new re/lease
on life

i remember
when my body knew
when it was time
to cry
and it was all
right then

to explode
the world
and melt
everything
warm

and start new
washed clean

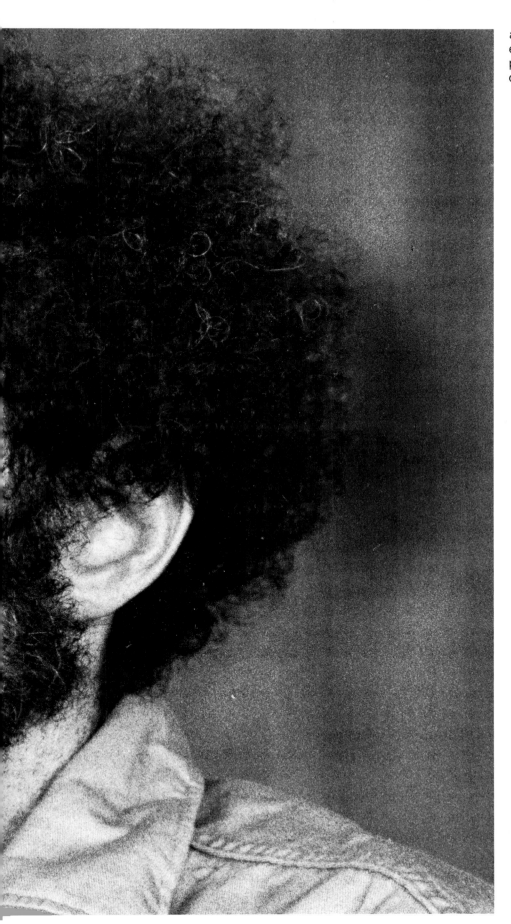

at the funeral
each friend
places a flower
on the coffin

after the funeral
a group of friends
gather together
and sit in a circle
and imagines
the dead person
in the center
one by one
each friend
tells the dead person
how he felt
about him
finishes any
unfinished business
and says good bye
to the being
that is
no more

a w

ake

after
there is
food
wine
dance

accept
dance

trance
end

dance

**peace
unearth**

there are
worlds
beyond universes
to which you
rarely allow your self
to travel

know there
go there
there there

come to

your the plan
it

x
to see

be aware

your there

hear it
see it
smell it
taste it
feel it
be it
all

you're the sun

you're the son

blessed

warm

eternal

one